Baby Boomer Reflections

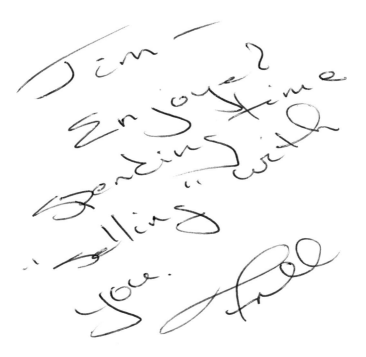

Baby Boomer Reflections

EIGHTEEN SPECIAL YEARS
BETWEEN 1946 AND 1964

Fred Arnow

ISBN: 1507830726
ISBN 13: 9781507830727
Library of Congress Control Number: 2015901789
CreateSpace Independent Publishing Platform
North Charleston, South Carolina

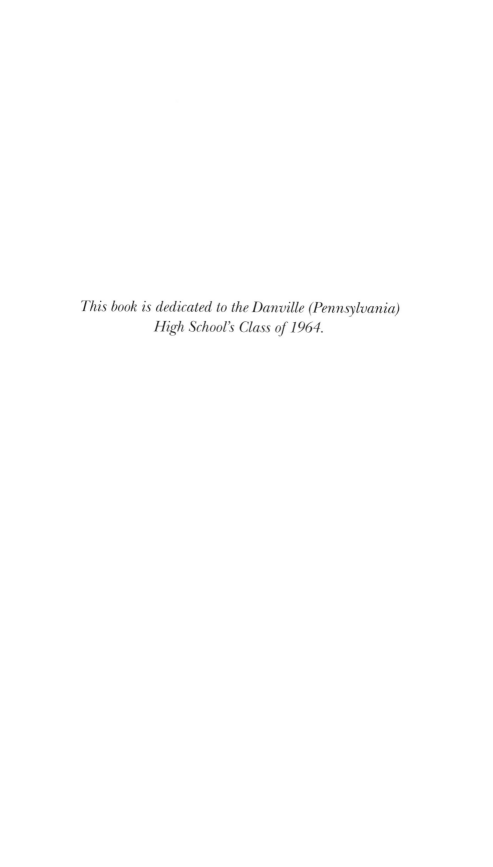

This book is dedicated to the Danville (Pennsylvania) High School's Class of 1964.

Contents

Acknowledgments

⸺⸻⸺

I WANT TO EXPRESS MY appreciation to Betsy, my lovely wife of forty-three years. She has inspired my creativity, allowed me to never grow up, and, at the same time, supported my efforts, no matter what they have been. We met in an officer's club in Norfolk, Virginia, when she was an elementary-school teacher and I was about to journey off to Southeast Asia aboard the USS *America* (CVA-66). After marriage, she traveled with me throughout the United States for corporate relocations, as we started our family. Betsy had her own three-decade public-education career in numerous school districts across America, and she finally retired to enjoy her new role as a grandmother.

I am also grateful to Mark Smith, PhD., Dean of Students at Dennison University and several other prestigious universities. Due to career changes, Mark and his wife, Nancy, moved from Granville, Ohio to Boulder, Colorado, into vacant student housing—coincidentally, right next door to Betsy and me. I had been ordered, as a naval officer, to the University of Colorado on temporary duty during the summer of 1972, after we were married, to train to become a Naval Reserve Officer Training Corps (NROTC) instructor. The four of us became fast friends. We've stayed in touch as both couples moved around the country. In 1997, I sent

Mark a copy of my first attempt to write a book. That literary effort ended abruptly when my computer crashed without backup, and I lost interest in trying to reconstruct my work. In early 2014, Mark found the copy I had sent him seventeen years earlier, and he returned it to me. He also said he had enjoyed reading it and encouraged me to write more. Mark's comment led me to this effort.

Finally, I want to mention two of my female classmates, but only by their first names, Judi and Judy. I reconnected with these two wonderful ladies during our high school's fiftieth class reunion. They both remained near the town where we had grown up, while I had journeyed far away. I shared my book idea with them and asked them to help me remember the way things were, and they responded with enthusiasm and advice. In addition, they were able to provide some gender balance to my myopic male views of growing up. They also went on road trips to discover information and to take some terrific photography. Many of Judy's photographs are in this book and many others are on babyboomerreflections.com.

"Memories Are Made of This," by Dean Martin

───◦≈≈◦───

IN 1956, THAT SONG REACHED number one on the *Billboard* chart and stayed there for six weeks. Isn't it amazing how songs can take you back to a particular time and place? I know you remember the words. Sweet memories that you can't beat. When you think back to that time, where were you? A quote from an unknown person says, "All it takes is one song to bring back a thousand memories." That's an understatement!

Memory begins at birth and is formed continuously thereafter. Memories start out in short-term storage and hopefully wind up in long-term storage. Although memory can be transferred from short- to long-term storage through repetitive action, it can also wind up there through association; in other words, sometimes you remember something because you associate it with something else. Things you enjoy and remember fondly are generally easier to put into your long-term bank. According to experts, lots of times a person doesn't even know what might be in the bank until it's needed for some reason, and suddenly that memory appears, seemingly without effort.

There are several types of memory, and the one this book is concerned with is episodic memory: the memory of times, places, and emotions—the who, what, where, when, and why that can be explicitly stated. It makes up the collection of past personal experiences that occurred at particular times and places.

Everyone has his or her individual memories, and these respective memories may or may not be interesting to anyone besides the individual. It's uncommon for multiple people to have similar memories. It's even more unusual for a large group of individuals to share similar memories from a similar perspective at a similar point in time, but there are exceptions.

This book is one of those unusual exceptions. It's about me. It's about you. It's about us, all of us, all seventy-six million American baby boomers. It's a collection of past personal experiences that occurred while we baby boomers were in our formative years, defined as those eighteen years between birth and graduation from high school.

No matter where your formative years happened, if you're a baby boomer, your memories will be similar, perhaps not in total, but certainly in part. These memories must be preserved, and they must be shared and passed on to your children, your grandchildren, and for those baby boomers who had their children early, your great-grandchildren. Now, that's a memory I didn't have. Reproductively speaking, I adapted long after others in that part of my life.

The high-school graduates of 1964 are the leading-edge boomers. Having been born in 1946, they have already had their fiftieth high school reunions. As a member of that august group, I participated in one of those high-school reunions and sat in on many conversations about what things were like "back then" during our formative years.

How did our towns, schools, and communities look and feel? Those conversations, questions, and thoughts led to this quest to research and attempt to rediscover certain simple things many of us might have failed to appreciate while they were actually happening. Certainly the incredible innovation and technological advances that we're experiencing today are vital in a dynamic society; yet, for some reason, the simplicity, safety, and security of the "good old days" are appealing. Having said that, I find it humorous to think that, someday, current times will be the good old days for another generation. The mid-1940s through the mid-1960s have been described in many ways: "traditional" seems to me to be the best fit. My mother used to remind me nearly every time we spoke that these days were the best of times. How I wished that I'd heeded her words.

So let's move on together, to a time unfortunately somewhat long ago, and see what memories of yours suddenly appear once they are stimulated by things you might discover in the following pages.

Fred Arnow

The House on Pine Street

——— ∞∞ ———

My TOWN BELONGED TO THE Iroquois Indians until a treaty in 1768 allowed for the ownership of land by the colonists, and a Revolutionary War figure purchased a parcel of land for a trading post. He built his house in 1792, and his son began to plot the land during that same year. Actually, my town is not really a town, but rather a borough, probably a holdover from its British roots. My borough was named after the purchaser's son.

As described in a book published in 1881, slightly more than a century after the plot of land was acquired, my borough was "situated on the right bank of the North Branch of the Susquehanna river about eleven miles above its confluence with the West Branch. It is surrounded by the most charming and picturesque scenery, and is nestled in a narrow valley, between Blue Hill and Montour Ridge. Tall hills, in their wild grandeur, and clad in their native robes of emerald, rise on every side, and down the pleasant vale, beyond the river, beautiful white cottages dot the landscape."

At one time, my borough had an asylum, an opera house, a great iron works, almost a score of churches and two thousand dwellings. As a strange coincidence, the borough's population

4

peaked in 1870 at 8,129, nearly concurrent with the aforementioned book's publishing. Ten years later, the borough's population was in decline to 7,698, and this population was dispersed almost equitably throughout the borough's four wards.

My 1.6-square-mile borough is in central Pennsylvania, and it's not unlike hundreds, if not thousands, of small centers of populations all over the United States, whether they are called boroughs, towns, villages, or cities. As previously stated, more than eight thousand people lived here in the late 1800s, but that number has been decreasing steadily since, due to industry migrations to other places. There are now about forty-five hundred people in the borough, and many of the old businesses that were on Mill Street years ago are now gone.

So, who am I? That will become evident shortly.

During the boom years, my borough became a transportation center with railroads, river barges, and a canal system. A large state hospital was built in 1869. In 1886, a free library and an attached YMCA became focal points of the community.

A borough resident who was born in 1817 and died in 1894 supervised the actual construction of the library and YMCA, both built of gray, Ohio stone with granite trimmings and Scottish-granite columns. He built me in about 1848, which should help identify what I am: I'm his house, and I'm still around. Like the library and YMCA, I'm proud to have been designated a historical site.

I remained with my builder's family until 1975, when I was sold to my current owner. For the next forty years, my new family spent a lot of time and loving care getting me into the shape I now appreciate.

So now that you know who I am, let's get back to the story. The story actually begins almost seventy years ago, in 1946 and 1947, when nearly seven thousand people still lived in the area. I know that sounds like ancient history to many of you, but it doesn't to me. For me, it's recent—almost current. After all, I'm about a century older than the story, and I can remember all of this like it just happened. I'm writing this book to commemorate life as I experienced it through people I've come to know since 1946, and, if you're part of that generation, you'll remember that life, too.

Are you ready to move forward?

"My Home Town," by Paul Anka

IT WAS A PLEASANT THURSDAY night in September 2014 when people started to gather for an event, as many had been doing for several months. In fact, some had been gathering for several years. They were coming to visit me, and I was about to enjoy another evening of camaraderie and merriment. The event was called "pizza night," but in fact, it was a get-together of classmates, specifically, the members of the Class of 1964, who had graduated from the high school named for the borough fifty years earlier.

Pizza night had evolved over the years, having originated with a group of local female classmates who now had free time available because their kids had grown up. These women would get together periodically to visit. In time other friends joined in, and soon even a few guys became a part of the group. Soon pizza night became a recurring monthly event, and it grew both in numbers of participants and in the support it provided to the attendees.

Some of the new attendees that September evening were from out of town, and they, like the protagonist in Paul Anka's song, had come back to the place where they had grown up. Some of them were from way out of town, or, should I say, out of the borough. Before I talk about my evening of eavesdropping, let me give you some background.

Back in about 1952, when these adults were mere kids, they started elementary school as first graders. They collectively would eventually become known as baby boomers. If you remember, I was born—or should I say constructed—in 1848, so I'm about one hundred years older than these baby boomers, who were just arriving on earth. World War II ended in 1945, and these babies were the progeny of the members of what would be known eventually as the Greatest Generation. Having saved the world from evil in the forms of Nazi Germany and imperial Japan, the new or soon-to-be new parents set about to rebuild an American economy and establish peace at home. They also procreated in record numbers. According to History.com,

> Almost exactly nine months after World War II ended, "the cry of the baby was heard across the land," as historian Landon Jones later described the trend. More babies were born in 1946 than ever before: 3.4 million, 20 percent more than in 1945. This was the beginning of the so-called "Baby

Boom." In 1947, another 3.8 million babies were born; 3.9 million were born in 1952; and more than 4 million were born every year from 1954 until 1964, 18 years later, when the boom finally tapered off. By then, there were 76.4 million baby boomers in the United States. They made up almost 40 percent of the nation's population.

The end of World War II began a new era, not only for America, but also for the entire world. It was a time of social conservatism and prosperity. Because of the war, hundreds of thousands of young men had been separated from their girlfriends and wives for years, and they were in a hurry to get married and begin their families.

If you are observant, you've already noticed that this baby boom started in 1946 and lasted eighteen years, until 1964. I've already assumed too much persona, and I don't want you to consider me a philosopher, but I have to point out the alpha (1946) and the omega (1964): the beginning and the end. The classmates I've referred to were there for all of it.

My visitors were baby boomers, actually, leading-edge baby boomers because most of them were born in 1946, with a few hanging in utero until early 1947. I'm going to consider them leading-edgers, too, because they graduated from high school in 1964. So on that September evening in 2014, they had stopped by to visit me the night before their fiftieth high-school reunion, which would be held over the next two days.

When my visitors graduated from high school, the Class of 1914, the year World War I began, would have been having its fiftieth reunion; and the seniors in that class would have been born in 1896. Is that bizarre? It isn't for me; I'm older than that. What could those members of the Class of 1914 have told these classmates if only these classmates had been prescient enough to ask? What could these Class of 1964 members share with their figurative descendants of 2014?

I don't know how many leading-edge baby boomers started in our borough's elementary schools in 1952, but I can tell you from historical data that 227 of them were promoted from my borough's junior-high school in 1961, and 196 of them graduated from my borough's high school in 1964. Sadly, about thirty-five have passed away. More than half of these remaining classmates still live within twenty miles of the borough. I'll bet their kids went to many of the same schools, and I'll also bet that many of their parents, members of the Greatest Generation, did so as well.

The baby boom certainly wasn't unique to my borough; it was happening all over the United States. These baby boomers have all grown up together, and they've all experienced many of the same things regardless of whether they were from a borough, a town, or a city. According to various sources, approximately eight to ten thousand boomers are currently turning sixty-five every day, and those who are retiring approximate the same daily number. Many of those retirees have moved to age-restricted communities. I'm obviously not a part of an age-restricted community, so I had to learn what that meant. Here's what I found: "Age-restricted" means you have to be at least fifty-five to be a resident. It also means that if you are a resident, you can go to early-bird specials. It's amazing how many folks are willing to eat dinner at 3:00 p.m. to save a few bucks! The downside is that the early birders then go to sleep at 8:00 p.m. and wake up at 4:00 a.m. I'm glad that I am not concerned with such routines.

So most of my visitors were regulars at pizza night, whereas a few new guests joined them that night in September 2014. One in particular was more of an outsider, having left the borough quickly after graduation. In that person's case, lots of introductions were necessary. Amazingly, the mere mention of a person's name elicited immediate recall, as if time had stood still and the group was back in high school. Obviously, a lot had changed for both my visitors and me, but the conversations flowed back to the way things were fifty or more years ago. Certain people recalled certain memories, whereas others shared different recollections, and it suddenly became obvious that it was simple things—things that caused the aforementioned person to quickly abandon the borough—that were unappreciated in their time, but were now remembered and craved by everyone. In a real sense, despite the incredible progress and innovation that has transpired at an ever-quicker pace subsequent to the baby boomers' graduations, there was a pervasive yearning to go back to the simplicity, security, and safety of the "good old days." There really was no consensus on a definition of what those days should be called now. Were they "simpler," "easier," "better"? I'm sticking with "traditional."

This, then, is my attempt to describe an America through the recollections and experiences of a few of my borough residents. I'm sure you will find similarities between them and yourself, especially if you went to Saturday movie matinees. No doubt, you also hurried home from school to see Spin and Marty on *The Mickey Mouse Club*, where you also learned how to spell "encyclopedia" because Jiminy Cricket taught you how. And I'm also reasonably certain you watched Dick Clark on *American Bandstand*. You probably practiced all the latest dances so you could show off the next time you had the chance.

Do you have any memories of the first few years of leading-edge baby-boomer life? Perhaps your memories are spurred by a photo, like the one found in my attic: that of a young boy standing near a curb watching a parade in about 1949, wearing a pith helmet and holding a baton. I'll bet he had no clue how his mom got him to wear a pith helmet. As you became older, your memories became more specific and also more similar to those of your peers.

Please allow me to introduce the concept that perception is reality. Simply stated, if you perceive it, it's real (at least to you). Consequently, everything I am going to tell you is the truth, at least in my mind. Let me enhance that a wee bit by quoting one of America's greatest philosophers, Yogi Berra, who was one heck of a great catcher as well. Of the many brilliant statements attributed to this genius, my favorite is, "I never said most of the things I said." That's my plan with regard to what I'm writing, too: If it's written here, you can count on its being accurate, even though I might not have said it originally.

Let me try to restate that in another way. Although much of what follows is true, please keep in mind some of the advice the media frequently offer to baby boomers: Memory starts to lapse slightly as one grows more mature. Do memory lapses therefore make this a work of fiction? Maybe they do a wee bit, but you'll never know where truth stops and fiction begins.

"America," by Neil Diamond

∽∽

ELLIS ISLAND, IN UPPER NEW York Bay, was the gateway to America for millions of immigrants like the travelers you can picture in the Neil Diamond anthem. The island's immigrant-inspection station opened in 1892 and continued to function until about 1954—coincidentally, about a third of the way through the baby boom. Many immigrants who came through Ellis Island learned English, became assimilated throughout the United States and settled in reasonably close proximity to their relatives and predecessors. That resulted in some stereotyping related to where certain groups lived.

Here's a little geography lesson about my borough: It was organized into four wards, creatively named First Ward, Second Ward, Third Ward, and Fourth Ward. It doesn't get more unique than that, does it? There is some debate about who moved into each of my borough's wards. Around the end of the nineteenth century, my borough had more than two thousand residents in each of its wards, except for Second Ward, which had around fourteen hundred residents. On one hand, it could have been that a scarcity of cars made it necessary for people to live close to where they worked because they might have to depend on their feet for transportation. (I believe that was called "walking.") Owning a car was definitely a luxury, and almost no households had more than one car; many households had none. Many women were homemakers who didn't even have driver's licenses. If a person was lucky, perhaps a bus might pass by that could take him or her close to a desired destination. On the other hand, perhaps people made the choice to live near friends and relatives or just people like themselves.

In any event, such was the case in my borough. First Ward residents were primarily professionals: store and office owners and the people who worked for them. Second Ward residents were factory and state-hospital workers, probably what are now referred to as "blue-collar" workers. Third Ward was where the former iron-mill employees lived, but that mill had long since closed. Surviving the closure were the bars and other hangouts where the men used to go to let off steam and spend some of their weekly earnings. In our Third Ward, the mill owners had constructed houses for their workers, and these mill homes were very simple wooden structures. Fourth Ward was home to employees of the borough's second hospital as well as to other residents who couldn't find a place to live in one of the other three wards. There were also outlying areas: two townships, a community on the other side of the river that bordered one side of the borough, and a farming community that was fairly distant from the population center. If you lived in the borough, your school(s), teachers, family, playground(s), and, ultimately, your identity reflected the ward where you grew up.

As a result of stereotyping based on where one lived, the classmates at the pizza party related pervasive attitudes they had absorbed from teachers and parents when they were younger: feelings of superiority or inferiority to others. Some of them felt pressure to avoid people from one area and to make friends with people from another area.

Those classmates whose parents were farmers had to return to their farms immediately after school to do their chores; therefore they seldom got to participate in after-school activities. It's surprising to hear them speak today about how they felt so isolated and excluded by their classmates, but, as I previously stated, perception is reality.

"To Each His Own," by Jay Livingston and Ray Evans

❦

THE BOOM BEGINS

*"I hate war as only a soldier who has lived it can, only as
one who has seen its brutality, its stupidity."*
DWIGHT D. EISENHOWER, January 10, 1946

AND SO BEGINS THE JOURNEY or, shall I say, the boom? How appropriate was the song, "To Each His Own?" Four different versions by four different artists were in the *Billboard* top 40, and three even hit number one at some point during the year. It was a wonderful love song in which lots of suggestions were made. And lots of GIs and their wives took them to heart.

The year 1946 began on a Tuesday, exactly 239 days after VE Day marked the end of World War II in Europe and 122 days after VJ Day marked the end of World War II in Japan. During that year, notable events included the following:

* A revival of *Showboat* opened on Broadway.
* The United Nations met for the first time.
* Ho Chi Minh signed an agreement with France that recognized Vietnam as an autonomous state.
* Tokyo Telecommunications Engineering (later renamed Sony) was founded with twenty employees.
* Bikinis went on sale in France.
* The US Atomic Energy Commission was established.
* Hermann Goering, founder of the Gestapo, poisoned himself two hours before his scheduled execution.
* UNICEF (UN International Children's Emergency Fund) was founded.

Note some other interesting facts: Federal spending was $55.23 billion, federal debt was $271 billion, unemployment was 3.9 percent, a first-class stamp cost $0.03, and the average cost of a gallon of gasoline was $0.21.

The top Academy Awards (the nineteenth annual ceremony, honoring 1946 releases) were as follows:

* Best Motion Picture: *The Best Years of Our Lives*
* Best Actor: Fredric March (*The Best Years of Our Lives*)
* Best Actress: Olivia de Havilland (*To Each His Own*)

Billboard's top-five songs of 1946 were as follows:

1. "Prisoner of Love," Perry Como
2. "To Each His Own," Eddy Howard
3. "The Gypsy," Ink Spots
4. "Five Minutes More," Frank Sinatra
5. "Rumors Are Flying," Frankie Carle

As you already know, 1946 was the first year of the infamous rise in births that ultimately came to be known as the baby boom. When the boomers started to arrive, the first males were frequently named after their fathers, so there were lots of youngsters who were referred to as "Junior." Adding a *y* after the last letter in some boy's name was also quite common. For example, Joey, Billy, Bobby and Freddy, to name just a few, became their respective nicknames. After emerging from two world wars and the Great Depression, it was a time to start celebrating, so names reflected things that gave their parents joy. For example, Lucille Ball helped to make mothers start to laugh again. Lucille therefore became a name of choice. Child stars, like Shirley Temple, Judy Garland,

and Margaret O'Brien, whose original name was Angela Maxine, were also name models, and Maxine became another favorite. There were lots of Larrys, a shortened version of the first name of actor Sir Laurence Olivier, and also Fredericks, with miscellaneous spellings to include or exclude the second *e* and the *k*. Fredric, with neither extra letter, was how Fredric March, who would win an Academy Award winner in the 1946 release *The Best Years of Our Lives*, actually spelled his name.

Among the 3.4 million boomers born in 1946 were several who would achieve significant subsequent fame, including Linda Ronstadt, Bill Clinton, Steven Spielberg, Freddie Mercury, Jimmy Buffett, Sylvester Stallone, Donald Trump, Dolly Parton, Diane Von Furstenberg, Lesley Gore (who passed away while I was writing this book), Gianni Versace, Liza Minnelli, and Diane Keaton, to name just a few.

After the war, gender roles for men and women were typically traditional and very well defined. For the most part, moms, who might have worked in the factories during the war to support the war effort, generally returned to and stayed home to raise their families, while dads worked to support the home economics. That dynamic stayed in place for many years until the women's liberation movement began in the late 1960s, but that's beyond the scope of this book.

Supermarkets as we know them today didn't exist, but nearly every neighborhood had a mom-and-pop store that sold staples like milk, bread, and eggs, along with penny candy, like Necco Wafers, Hershey Kisses, bubble gum cigars, candy cigarettes, licorice and jawbreakers, to keep the kids happy. There were some butcher shops where the city folks got their meat, and if you lived on one of the many farms throughout the community, you had your livestock killed and butchered periodically to meet the family's needs. Similarly, the farmers sold their abundant crops at produce stands or regular weekly farmers' markets.

Milk was delivered to front porches in glass bottles with collectible tops sealed with wax. After the milk was consumed, the bottles were washed, cleaned, and returned to the front porch to be replaced on a subsequent delivery by the milkman. Specialty products like chocolate milk, buttermilk, and cream had to be ordered in advance. Notes to the milkman, for special orders and changes in future quantities, were left in the empty bottles. The milk was delivered cold, and it had to be brought into the house soon after its delivery lest it freeze in the winter or go sour in the summer. All the milk was fresh and preservative-free. The milkman was generally recognizable from his uniform, dependable timing and the clattering of the glass bottles in their metal crates.

A variety of salesmen frequently knocked at the front door. They were selling things like vacuum cleaners, encyclopedias and consumer goods. One of the more recognized salesmen was the Fuller Brush Man. Nearly every week or on a frequent schedule, he came to deliver products or to drop off samples, fully expecting to make a sale on a followup call the next time he was there. In addition to the best brushes and brooms, Fuller had wonderful cleaning products and cosmetic items as well. Women weren't hired to work for Fuller until the company added their cosmetic line. Prior to that, women commonly went door-to-door selling Avon products.

Almost every town had a daily newspaper that was released in the morning and delivered mostly by "paperboys" and a few "papergirls" (as opposed to "news carriers") who had coveted paper routes. These entrepreneurs had to get up early and go to a distribution point to collect their supplies of newspapers for their respective routes. In order to facilitate the delivery of papers to front porches, newspapers could be rolled up and folded in a certain way so that they could be assembled in a bag and then thrown appropriately at their destinations. When a bad throw happened, the paperboy or papergirl had to stop, retrieve the paper, and place it where it needed to be. Some routes could be walked, whereas other longer ones were managed from the seat of a bicycle.

Periodically, usually once a week on a specific day, the paper-boy or papergirl had to visit houses twice, once to deliver the paper in the morning, and then again in the afternoon to collect payment for the papers. The customer would have a coupon book that would be paper-punched to signify that payment had been made for the week(s) in question. The money would be brought to the newspaper supplier, who would extract an appropriate wholesale amount to for the papers and hand over the excess as pay to the paperboy or papergirl. The borough also had a store where news-papers from big cities like New York City and Philadelphia would be delivered via a Greyhound bus, and residents could purchase these papers directly from the store. There was certainly a lot more information in the big newspapers, but the critically important stuff, like local sports-team scores, births, marriages, and deaths were the mainstays of the community papers. Other important community events like meetings of the Cub Scouts, Girl Scouts, or the 4H Club, never seemed to be covered by the *New York Times* or the *Philadelphia Inquirer.*

Houses were small, especially when you considered the number of kids in a typical family. Many households had five or more children, and these kids shared bedrooms, small closets, and possibly only one bathroom for the entire family. Baths were taken in tubs, and most tubs didn't have a fixed shower or a handheld attachment.

Breakfast was a family event unless the dads had already left for work. Breakfast food was stuff that moms said would "stick to your ribs." That must have been important, because breakfast was often quite a hearty meal. Dishes were quietly taken to the sink after the food was eaten and the rib-sticking had begun. Without dishwashers, every pot, pan, plate, and piece of silverware had to be washed and dried by hand, and then placed back in the cupboard to await its next use.

Dinner was frequently called "supper," and it was when the entire family sat down as a group to enjoy a sumptuous meal, typically cooked by a talented mom. Divorces didn't happen much in those days, so there weren't too many single-parent homes. While the family sometimes sat together for breakfast, too, depending on school start times, and when a parent had to be at work, supper was special. Lots of moms were first- or second-generation Americans, so meals prepared by them frequently resembled meals from their own backgrounds. As an example, if your mom had a Pennsylvania Dutch heritage, you ate a lot of Pennsylvania Dutch dishes, like beef potpie and homemade bread. There were quite a few families whose relatvies came from eastern Europe, especially Poland, so there were lots of meals that featured sauerkraut, pierogis, kielbasa, golumpkis and cabbage soup.

In many homes, food selections were frequently timed around the father's pay cycle. For example, the night before pay day, supper might consist of a nutritious soup the contents of which might be what was left over from previous meals. Another night-before-payday dinner might have a meat with beans to make it go further. Very soon after the paycheck was received the kids might be treated to ice cream for desert.

When children came home from school, the house was filled with certain smells, especially that of baked bread, and baby boomers can still remember those aromas with great love and affection. Memories of those smells still evoke occasional tears when adult boomers experience olfactory recall. Seldom did baby boomers eat out in restaurants—possibly not until they were teenagers. No one used paper plates or plastic utensils. Meals were served on china, and drinks were served in glasses. Sometimes, the glasses were actually empty jelly jars.

Although the following certainly isn't universal, it's definitely representative of a typical supper. When a dad came home from work, the family was expected to be ready to sit down and eat together. Many times, the dad would read the daily paper while they ate. There was no arguing or roughhousing because those activities could result in dad glaring over the top of the paper, and this was something no kid wanted to experience. The kids and their mom exchanged small talk until the dad was ready to enter the conversation.

Whatever was prepared for dinner was what everyone ate. You could make requests, but if you came home and smelled a cabbage dish, liver and onions, or fried chicken, you were either going to eat what was served or be hungry that night. If there was a dessert, it was a very special treat; desserts weren't served much. There were very few boxed or frozen meals. Almost everything was prepared from scratch, and moms (typically) were almost universally great cooks and innovators.

When the temperatures began to drop, most heating came from coal-burning furnaces. Coal was ordered and delivered either in a pile outside the house, or via a chute that led to a storage place usually inside a dirt-floor basement. After the coal had been burned, its ash needed to be shoveled outside for disposal. Ash was a great source of friction to allow cars to move when snow or ice made the roads slippery. Standing on one of the floor grates was a wonderful way to warm up after coming home from a day at school or from playing on the weekend. The forced air was nice and toasty, and sometimes, houses like me, would creak from expansion as the interior temperature rose.

Suppertime, which was fairly predictable and rigidly observed, trumped playtime, and kids had to be home. Most neighbors knew each other, and parents looked out for both their children and their neighbors' kids. After supper, the neighborhood kids would convene for games like hide-and-go-seek; kick the can; Wiffle ball; red rover, red rover; jacks; marbles; or reliever. These games were universal, required little to no equipment, and were loads of fun. If you were lucky, you might have access to a pair of metal-wheel skates that you would step into while wearing your shoes, and then use a skate key to tighten up the clamps, which made your shoes a part of the skates or vice versa. It took some effort to get good at skating, and some of the neighborhood kids became quite proficient and were the envy of other kids on the block. In the summer, catching lightning bugs was in vogue, along with capturing night crawlers after they came to the surface following a good rain. A yet-to-be invented toy would soon dominate every street throughout the nation. That toy, the Hula-Hoop, would be invented in 1958 by Wham-O, but at this time, it was still unknown.

In the wintertime, riding sleds was a popular activity, especially on days when school had been called off because of snow. Lots of kids had Lightening Glider sleds, and they rode them on any hill they could find. The sleds were made in a factory near the Pennsylvania state capitol and were shipped all over the US. When ponds or the river froze over, skating happened.

At least one evening a week, families would try to sit together to play a board game. The games were designed for specific age groups. I frequently eavesdropped on my kids playing Candy Land, Checkers, Chutes and Ladders, Cootie and other games that looked like a lot of fun. There was always lots of laughter.

In 1946, after a four-year suspension during World War II, the All-American Soap Box Derby resumed for young boys to exhibit their mechanical and driving skills in local races held all over America. Sponsored by Chevrolet, these soap-box races were an event around which entire communities could rally to cheer on their boys to victory. Local winners might advance all the way to Akron, Ohio, for the national finals. Twenty-five years later, the Derby would be opened to girls, and four years after that, in 1975, a girl became the national champion.

Sugared soft drinks existed back then, but they didn't come in a lot of varieties. Depending on where you grew up, these drinks might have been called soda or pop. They came in small bottles, and the bottles had to be returned in order to reclaim a bottle deposit. A case of drinks consisted of twenty-four bottles in a wooden box. The mainstays then were 7UP, Coca-Cola, Pepsi-Cola, Hires, and Squirt. Before the 1950s, the typical bottle size was 6.5 ounces, and in the 1960s that size increased to 12 ounces. In the late 1950s, a new company created a drink called Lotta Cola, a virtual behemoth at 16 ounces. If your parents didn't want to buy the bottled drinks, they could use a popular drink mix called Kool-Aid to make up their own pitchers.

If my kids were lucky, they might occasionally hear tinny amplified music coming from a refrigerated specialty truck. It was the ice-cream man, used interchangeably with the Good Humor man. In the 50s, there weren't lots of choices offered by the ice-cream man. As I remember, he sold only a three-ounce chocolate-coated vanilla ice cream bar on a stick. In years to come, I watched my kids ponder over a huge variety of frozen treats with unique and comical names. Popsicle sticks became collectibles and could be used by creative kids to make crafty things.

Like many of my neighboring homes, I had a front porch, and many frequent and pleasant baby boomer evenings were spent sitting right there as we enjoyed afternoons and evenings together. The porch became a transitional space between the private world of the family and the public realm of the street. Porches became a necessity before air conditioning, whether it was the screened sleeping porch or the broad, columned veranda where iced tea — and gossip — were plentiful.

In the 1950s and 1960s, when families like mine had a front porch, they would sit on the porch in the evening. Neighbors, who were taking an evening stroll, would walk past and stop to talk and perhaps be invited to come and sit and visit. Young couples, that didn't have a car, would walk to their destination. All the neighbors would greet them as they walked past, and then the "porch sitter" would report on the couple to the next neighbor. Those boys who had cars would cruise up and down the streets in hopes the girls would be "porch sitting." What might happen afterwards is pure speculation and faded memory.

As Americans became more affluent, manufacturers of all types competed for their share of the consumer's wallet. Advertising was principally in print; television was still a relatively insignificant medium. There was quite a lot of information communicated in the printed ads. Put another way, baby boomers and their families had to read a lot of words to understand a product's features and benefits and why they should buy it. Image ads featured celebrities such as Sid Caesar, Ronald Reagan, John Wayne, and Rock Hudson and contained a lot of stereotypes about gender, role models, and lifestyles.

Automobile ads were upbeat. They featured lots of family photos in action scenarios along with their convertibles and stylized station wagons. Those ads were dominated by photographs rather than text, and the cars were generally shown in bright colors, especially red, yellow, green, and blue.

Those ads were tame compared to how other products were represented, though. What do you think of these beauties that ran in magazines and newspapers throughout the country?

"He wears the cleanest shirts in town...his 'Missus' swears by TIDE!"
I wonder if the rest of the family gets clean shirts as well.

"Christmas morning, she'll be happier with a Hoover [vacuum]."
Quite personal, right?

"Don't worry, darling, you didn't burn the Schlitz beer!"
Quite a backhanded compliment, don't you think?

"So the harder a wife works, the *cuter* she looks."
That certainly would make a woman want to eat Kellogg's
Pep cereal, wouldn't it?

"Blow in her face, and she'll follow you anywhere,"
advises Tipalet. But what if she doesn't like cigar smoke?

Del Monte ketchup displayed its latest bottle in the hands
of a surprised-looking woman with the slogan, "You mean a
woman can open it?"

And our future president, Ronald Reagan, frequents the scene
as he is "sending Chesterfields to all his friends. That's the merri-
est Christmas any smoker can have—Chesterfield mildness plus
no unpleasant aftertaste." At the same time, he declares that Van
Heusen Century shirts won't wrinkle ever, and that's why they're
"the neatest Christmas gift of all!" So which product did he really
give as gifts?

Finally, one of my favorites from the R. J. Reynolds Tobacco
Company claims, "According to a recent nationwide survey: More
Doctors Smoke Camels than Any Other Cigarette! Family physi-
cians, surgeons, diagnosticians, nose and throat specialists, doctors in every branch of medicine…a total of 113,597 doctors…were
asked the question: 'What cigarette do you smoke?' And more
of them named Camel as their smoke than any other cigarette!
Three independent research groups found this to be a fact. You
see, doctors, too, smoke for pleasure. That full Camel flavor is just
as appealing to a doctor's taste as to yours…that marvelous Camel
mildness means just as much to his throat as to yours. Next time,
get Camels. Compare them in your 'T-Zone' 30-day test." This ad
ran consistently until 1952.

The Leading-Edge Baby Boomers Start School

"I have no special talents. I am only passionately curious."
ALBERT EINSTEIN, March 11, 1952

THE YEAR 1952 WAS A leap year, and, like 1946, it also started on a Tuesday. Three out of five American families owned a car, two out of three families had a telephone, and one out of three homes had a television. The average American woman was married by age twenty and would not work after having children.

During that year, notable events included the following:

* Elizabeth II was crowned Queen of England.

* Wernher von Braun published the first in his series of articles titled "Man Will Conquer Space Soon."
* The B52 Stratofortress flew for the first time.
* The US Special Forces were created.
* General Dwight D. Eisenhower defeated Adlai Stevenson in the presidential election.
* Twelve-year-old Jimmy Boyd's record of "I Saw Mommy Kissing Santa Claus" sold three million records.
* Nearly fifty-eight thousand cases of polio were reported in the United States.

We can count among other interesting facts that federal spending was $67.69 billion, the federal debt was $259.1 billion, unemployment was 3.3 percent, a first-class stamp still cost $0.03, and the average cost for a gallon of gasoline was $0.20 to $0.25.

The top Academy Awards (the twenty-fifth annual ceremony, honoring 1952 releases) were as follows:

* Best Motion Picture: *The Greatest Show on Earth*
* Best Actor: Gary Cooper (*High Noon*)
* Best Actress: Shirley Booth (*Come Back, Little Sheba*)

Billboard's top-five songs were as follows:

1. "Blue Tango," Leroy Anderson
2. "Wheel of Fortune," Kay Starr
3. "You Belong to Me," Jo Stafford
4. "Auf Wiedersehen, Sweetheart," Vera Lynn
5. "Half as Much," Rosemary Clooney

In 1952, the leading-edge baby boomers were turning six, and they were ready to start elementary school. There weren't many opportunities for my children—that's how I think of them—to start their education before going to public school. Preschool was a thing whose time had not yet arrived, and kindergartens were few and far between. In the borough, a kindly woman, her sister, and her brother lived in one of the large houses near the river and operated a small private kindergarten named after the woman who owned the house. A few kids attended; four-year-olds went in the morning, and five-year-olds went in the afternoon. For most baby boomers, public first grade and, in some cases, private, religious first grade was the first opportunity to begin a twelve-year education.

I've already shared with you that the borough, where we learned reading, writing and 'rithmetic, was divided into four wards. I'm located in the borough's First Ward. Each of the wards had its own elementary school, and each of these schools handled about 150 pupils in six grades. My borough also had three other elementary schools that were physically located outside of the borough, but within the county. During those "School Days, School Days, Dear Old Golden Rule Days," my kids usually walked to their respective schools until they were old enough to ride their bikes. They could leave their unlocked bikes in a bike stand and not have to worry about anyone taking their bikes while they were in class. Some of the kids who lived a little too far away to walk got to ride a school bus, but very few kids were dropped off at school by their parents. Typically, boys read comic books and science fiction; girls played with Hula-Hoops after they had been invented. Both boys and girls enjoyed wearing blue jeans as a fashion statement.

Our elementary schools were old, and some of them didn't have enough rooms for each grade to have its own, so teachers had mixed classes. For example, a four-room school might have a room for first graders, another room for sixth graders, a room that had both second and fifth graders, and another for third and fourth graders. Of course, there were other permutations, including some one-room schoolhouses left over from previous generations. The principal was also a classroom teacher.

Each classroom had wooden desks with tops that generally lifted upward on hinges to reveal storage where school supplies could be kept. Lots of former students had carved their initials into the desks. Those indentations were a problem when you were writing on a piece of paper because, all of a sudden, you'd have a hole in your paper when the pencil tip went into a groove on the desktop. Older (wooden) desktops had holes that used to hold inkwells; some of the desks still had the actual inkwells, tops included, but no ink. I heard stories of kids catching flies in their hands and putting the flies into the inkwells. I guess it was almost like keeping a pet on your desk.

The year was divided into six, six-week periods. If you attended school around here, you would get a handwritten report card, signed by your teacher, to take home at the end of each period so that your parent could see how you were doing and sign off on it. You had to return the report card to the teacher in order to start the next six-week period. Occasionally, a pupil might try to forge a parent's signature, but that almost never slipped by the teacher. Marks were given for attendance and for good conduct or "deportment." At the end of a school year, a pupil either passed to the next grade or was held back to repeat the grade again. Social promotion wasn't practiced.

Each school year generally started in early September and lasted into mid-June of the following year. There were planned breaks for major holidays and special events, and there were unplanned breaks for severe weather, primarily snow. You already know that my borough was in rural America. Scheduled breaks included days off for the first days of small-game and large-game hunting season as well as for the first day of trout-fishing season. Many of my boys went hunting and fishing with their dads regularly, and quite a few of them even owned their own guns.

Every school day would start with a routine that would become quite familiar by the time you finished public education. That routine always included placing your hand over your heart and reciting the Pledge of Allegiance, and then bowing your head while you recited the Lord's Prayer. Elementary-school kids also had periodic drills to learn how to get under their school desks in case of an atomic-bomb attack. Another routine was reading and discussing the *Weekly Reader*, a kids' newspaper that I believe was required and was not free. I also heard that periodically my kids were given the opportunity to buy, for about a quarter, the names and addresses of potential pen pals who lived in Europe, wherever that was. I'm sure the people who had gathered those names had nothing but good intentions about my kids interacting with new "friends" from foreign lands, but I'm told that few of those European kids ever wrote back. Perhaps their addresses were bad.

At the start of each six-week period, pupils would be given a new paper tablet and a new pencil. Until fourth grade, the tablets had extra space between the lines, and the pencils were thick, but when pupils got to fourth grade, grown-up-looking tablets and number-two wooden pencils with erasers on top were the reward. There were pencil sharpeners at the front of the each room, and one lucky kid per class had the responsibility of emptying the pencil sharpener when it got full. Lots of time was spent on a class called penmanship. That class was designed to teach pupils how to write cursive. The kids spent a considerable amount of time doing exercises, that is, tracing circles or lines consecutively on their tablets. The transition from printing to cursive didn't start until fourth grade, when, again, the tablet lines got smaller and the pencils more dainty. In other words, it would have been easier if you could have used the little kids' tablets with the bigger lines. At times, cursive writing, I'm told, was more like drawing than writing because the students made circles and continuous lines rather than letters. But these exercises only lasted until the pupils had to actually start writing letters that were connected to one another.

Every classroom had real blackboards, made of whatever real blackboards came from—probably sheets of slate—and a lot of chalk, including a few sticks of colored chalk. Some kids had the responsibility of washing the blackboards at the end of the day. There was nothing worse than a dirty blackboard. There was also nothing worse than a piece of chalk making a screeching noise on the blackboard, but I don't think that had anything to do with whether the blackboard was clean or not. It had more to do with how the person, who was writing on the blackboard, actually held the piece of chalk, but now I'm digressing. By the way, the kids' blackboards were actually black, not green or gray or white.

The only other regular employee of a school beside its teachers and principal was its janitor, and he—it was always a man—was sometimes more important than the teachers. He kept the school clean and organized and was always on the spot to clean up after a sick pupil. He also burned the daily trash in an open fire pit near the playground. After a fire cooled off, it was always fun to see if there was any pencil lead left in the ashes. Pencil lead never burned, no matter how hot the fire was. Kids who were lucky enough to find pieces of lead could use them for writing, but they always had filthy hands afterward.

There were generally two recesses, one in the morning and one in the afternoon, and there was a lunch period during which everyone ate at the same time in their respective classrooms. There were no cafeterias in the borough schools until the new high school was built in the early sixties, so everyone had to bring their own lunches. Lunch buckets were must-have accessories, although some of the pupils preferred bags. There were boy- and girl-oriented lunch buckets. There were big-kid lunch buckets that looked like the ones their fathers took with them to work. The lunch buckets had thermoses that supposedly kept hot liquids hot and cold liquids cold. (I often wondered how thermoses knew how to do that, but I never got the answer.) One thing I knew about a thermos was that when it fell on the floor, something very fragile—probably the brain that knew whether to retain cold or heat—would break, and the contents couldn't be consumed. When a thermos broke, it was a sad day for its owner.

Once in a while, a school nurse would show up unannounced, and the kids were directed to one of two places for an exam. If they went to the room with windows, the nurse was going to check their teeth. If they went to the room without windows, generally the basement with the dirt floor, the nurse was going to turn out all the lights, turn on her special light with a strange black bulb that made the color white stand out, and carefully check out each kid's head for lice. Perhaps that happened because powerful shampoos hadn't yet been invented. Perhaps it was that the school's principal had acquired the black light from a war-surplus store and had to justify its purchase. If you remember, few houses had showers, so you had to wash your hair in the bathtub or over the sink. I wonder if more kids' teeth or heads were saved as a result of these hygiene inspections, but, once again, I digress.

When my kids started third grade, America started to fight back against terrifying outbreaks of poliomyelitis, or polio for short. Doctor Jonas Salk, a Pittsburgh physician, developed a vaccine delivered via injection to combat the highly contagious disease, and mass inoculations began. There was a high success rate, and new polio cases dropped by nearly two-thirds by the time my kids had made it to fifth grade.

You know that my borough had a hospital, but when the kids got sick, it was quite common for a physician to make a house call if it was too difficult to bring the child to the physician's office. The doctors who made these house calls were as identifiable in their own way as were the milkmen. A doctor would show up at a home, wearing a suit and carrying a bag, generally a black, leather valise, that contained a stethoscope, an otoscope, loads of tongue depressors that looked like oversized Popsicle sticks, and whatever injection the doctor figured would be necessary to cure the illness of the day.

In these years, the very few homes that actually had telephones had black devices that were simply handsets resting on top of bases. When you picked up the handset, you would hear a disembodied voice—almost always that of a woman—say, "Number, please?" Callers were supposed to respond with the phone numbers they wished to call. One of my numbers was 468M. I shared it with an office, and the office's number was 468J. A caller who was really cool would just say "M" or "J" when the voice asked, and somehow the voice knew to connect the caller with the other side of the phone pair.

Many families had party lines, which meant that several homes shared the same phone trunk. It was important for people to know when they were calling party lines because they would need to keep those conversations short, especially if a nasty person lived in one of the houses on the shared phone trunk and enjoyed yelling at another person who was on the phone too long in another house. In fact, anyone who wanted to could listen to someone else's conversation. Unless the person who was listening made a noise, the people having a conversation were unaware of the eavesdropper. In retrospect, I'm sure some eavesdroppers heard some crazy conversations.

The women who connected the phone calls were called "telephone operators," or "operators" for short, and this was a large career field for women who wanted or needed to work during the early fifties. They would stick plugs into open sockets, and—bam!—calls were made. If you needed to call a person in a different community, it was called a long-distance call, and it was very expensive. The Bell Telephone Company owned all the equipment involved, including the handsets that were located in the houses and offices. Users paid a rental fee each month for the privilege of having a phone to use. Telephone operators were important until community phone systems embraced local switching. Local switching enabled rotary dials to be included on the actual telephones, and the users were able to make calls independently. As dial phones entered communities, operators disappeared. The three- or four-position alphanumeric system was replaced with a somewhat complicated system that initially consisted of a word and five numbers but eventually transitioned into seven digits. For example, the borough's phone numbers consisted of "Browning," the number five, and then four more numbers. The prefix Browning, which was actually represented by just the letters "B" and "R" later became the number two (for "B"), the number seven (for "R"), five, and so forth.

In the early 1950s, television was starting to have an impact on the nation. To watch TV, your community had to be close enough to one of the growing number of stations that were developing throughout the country, and your household had to be able to afford a set. Broadcast initially only in black and white, commercial television became available with very limited programming. If regular programming wasn't scheduled, the local stations would broadcast "test patterns," and people frequently found themselves staring at these fixed images as if they could magically induce their TV sets to start playing real programs.

Early programming included shows like *The Texaco Star Theater*, starring Milton Berle, or *The Howdy Doody Show*, a kids' show. There were generally two fifteen-minute newscasts aired every day. Camel cigarettes sponsored NBC's John Cameron Swayze, one of the first featured newscasters in the business, and he was required to always have a burning cigarette visible when he was on camera. The number of television sets in use rose from about six thousand in 1946 to some twelve million by 1951. No new invention entered American homes faster than the black-and-white television set; by 1955, half of all US homes had one.

If you were lucky enough to live close to a TV transmitter, you only needed a set of "rabbit ears" (an antenna) on top of the TV set to receive a signal, but most families weren't that lucky. More typically, outside antennas were needed to get those broadcast signals, and many household heads spent hours erecting antenna towers in their yards or attaching devices to the roofs of their houses to allow this new medium to entertain their families. They also spent lots of time trying to point their directional antennas in order to maximize TV-signal strength. If a house was near several TV transmitters, the antenna had to be reoriented to get the alternate signals. In those cases, an antenna rotor, a mechanical device to turn the antenna in different directions, might have been necessary. It was a better solution than climbing up a tower to manually move the antenna, and then returning to the house to see if the move worked. It was quite possible for an antenna system to cost more than the actual TV set.

A particularly memorable TV event was the first nationwide broadcast of an atomic-bomb detonation over Nevada's Yucca Flat on Tuesday, April 22, 1952. These atom-bomb tests recurred throughout the remainder of the 1950s, and were one of many reasons that my kids practiced the emergency drills of taking shelter under their school desks, as I said before.

Almost concurrent with the arrival of TVs in houses came the famous TV dinners, and the odors that were enjoyed so much disappeared on those nights that moms decided to heat some of those infamous frozen dinners instead of cooking another meal. Swanson Foods was credited with launching the product in 1953 when it was stuck with a huge surplus of turkeys after poor Thanksgiving sales. Swanson packaged its leftover turkey with cornbread dressing, frozed peas and sweet potatoees in an aluminum tray that could be taken out of its frozen box and heated directly in the oven for twenty-five minutes at four hundred twenty fine degrees, and then consumed from the same tray. A turkey dinner cost ninety-eight cents. So families could now save time cooking dinners, and that meant more time for watching television. I'm told that most families were consuming at least one of these meals every week. The

TV dinner gave housewives, who were the family cooks, more free time for activities, both leisure and work, while at the same time, allowing them to give their families a hot meal.

Some elementary-school kids had fathers who were serving in the military during the Korean War between 1950 and 1953. As in World War II, when the fathers were off fighting, their wives maintained homelife and kept the kids on task. When the fighting ended, each of these men returned home to the same type of hero's welcome as had their predecessors in World War II. Many boys had Eisenhower jackets, modeled after the jacket worn by the famous general/President, and they proudly wore those jackets every time there was a parade to celebrate the veterans' homecoming.

During the summers, many of the schools kept their facilities open as local activity centers. In some communities, there were also playgrounds where kids could gather to play games with their friends. A highlight of the summer season at some of the playgrounds was when the staff would stage a "Tom Thumb" wedding during which the kids would all dress up and one boy and one girl would get to be the bride and groom.

Baseball seemed to be a boy's all-consuming hobby in spring and summer. All that was necessary for a pickup ball game were some guys and occasionally some girls who liked to play baseball, a wooden bat, some gloves, and a ball. Rocks were frequently used as bases. Most of the baseballs were inexpensive and had been hit so many times that their covers had been knocked off. Those baseballs were simply recovered with electrical tape and used over and over again. There were actually rubber-coated hardballs, but nobody liked to use them.

Football was the less-consuming hobby of fall, and basketball occupied winter and early spring until it was, once again, time for baseball. There were no distractions like soccer, volleyball, water polo, and so on, mostly because small-town kids hadn't even heard of these sports.

To expand on baseball, in the fifties, there were only sixteen major-league teams in ten cities. It was easy to follow team standings and favorite players until 1958, when the Brooklyn Dodgers and the New York Giants moved to the West Coast and triggered a series of events that pressured owners into the first of five expansions that would ultimately add fourteen teams to the league. While baseball cards featuring photographs of players had been around for more than a century, it wasn't until the early 1950s that Topps Chewing Gum Company issued its large, colorful cards. Six collector cards came in each package, which cost a nickel and included a large piece of pink bubble gum. There were cards for every major league player, and these cards were numbered so that they could be collected in series and sets. Multiple sets were released during a particular season. Boys and girls together collected the cards and chewed lots of gum in pursuit of completing an entire series of cards. Duplicate cards were exchanged and traded, almost like currency, and unwanted cards were frequently woven into spokes of bicycles to add either noise or personalization to a kid's bike. At the time, no one probably suspected the incredible value that these cards might bring to future investors. They were just toys.

Buses dominated intercity transportation, and the Greyhound Company was the largest of a number of competitors. The interstate highway system began in about 1956, and buses provided the opportunity for people to travel throughout the United States even if they didn't have their own automobiles. A little earlier, Greyhound had pioneered its exclusive Scenicruiser, a two-level behemoth that quickly became an icon of the American way of life. Scenicruisers even had onboard toilets. Travelers on the Scenicruiser didn't have to worry about drinking too much when the bus stopped at a rest stop because they knew they could relieve themselves en route.

The Greyhounds were driven by an esteemed group of professionals who wore giant sunglasses and very cool uniforms. Those heroes seemingly knew every waitress at all the stops, especially the Howard Johnson restaurants, because they had the menus memorized and therefore got served first. They also had the coolest hole punches on earth, that they used to punch passengers' tickets, and their hole punches were much better than the ones used by the neighborhood kids who delivered newspapers.

In the early 1950s, four airlines—American, United, Eastern, and TWA—dominated air travel in America. Propellers powered all commercial airplanes, and very few models were equipped for international flights. Although there were many airports throughout the country, most were small and had short runways; in fact, many had grass landing spots, so these commercial airliners operated from primarily large cities that provided manmade surfaces. Jet propulsion didn't arrive until the mid-1950s. Very few baby boomers even got to see a commercial airplane as children. But there was a small regional airport not too far from my borough, and so it wasn't uncommon for my families to drive to the airport to watch airliners land and take off.

YOUNG BOOMERS HAD HOUSEHOLD ASSIGNMENTS that they called chores, and these were faithfully performed so that mom or dad would pay an allowance, perhaps a dime, a quarter or fifty cents. One of those chores was helping their moms with the household's laundry. During these times, very few of the homes had a dryer. Most moms had only wringer-washers that sat in the corner of their kitchen. Those wringer-washers had a washer and two tubs for rinsing. After agitating in the soapy washtub, the clothes had to be removed from the washer, put through an attached wringer and then placed in a rinse tub. The wringer then swiveled, and the clothes were taken out of the rinse tub and put through the wringer again. And then, the clothes went into the second rinse tub, and the process repeated itself again, except this time, the clothes wound up in a basket to be taken outside to dry. The clean clothes were hung outside on clotheslines using clothespins. If the outside temperature was below freezing, the clothes were brought into the house, and they were stiff as a board. The now frozen laundry was hung over furniture to thaw out and finish drying. Everything got ironed including pillowcases and sheets. There was another machine that I remember, a mangle. The mangle was meant for ironing large items like sheets and tablecloths. It was a scary device, and it took up a lot of space.

The Leading-Edge Baby Boomers Go to Junior High

"Just because your voice reaches halfway around the world doesn't mean you are wiser than when it reached only to the end of the bar."
EDWARD R. MURROW, October 15, 1958

THE YEAR 1958 STARTED ON a Wednesday. During that year, notable events included the following:

* Sputnik 1 fell to earth from its orbit and burned up.

- Hall of Fame baseball player Roy Campanella was involved in an automobile accident that ended his career and left him paralyzed.
- The first successful American satellite, Explorer 1, was launched into orbit.
- The US Army inducted Elvis Presley as a private.
- Nikita Khrushchev became premier of the Soviet Union.
- Fidel Castro's revolutionary army began its attacks on Havana.
- Pizza Hut was founded.
- The first Datsun was sold just a few months after the first Toyopet, the name of Toyota's first of several models commercially available in the US, was sold late in the prior year.
- The US Congress formally created the National Aeronautics and Space Administration (NASA).

It was also interesting that federal spending was $82.41 billion; the federal debt was $279.7 billion; unemployment was 4.3 percent; and a first-class stamp still cost $0.03 until August 1, 1958, when it went up to $0.04. The average cost for a gallon of gasoline was $0.24.

The top Academy Awards (the thirty-first annual ceremony, honoring 1958 releases) were as follows:

- Best Motion Picture: *Gigi*
- Best Actor: David Niven (*Separate Tables*)
- Best Actress: Susan Hayward (*I Want to Live!*)

Billboard's top-five songs of 1958 were as follows:

1. "Volare," Domenico Modugno
2. "All I Have to Do Is Dream," Everly Brothers

3. "Don't/I Beg of You," Elvis Presley
4. "Witch Doctor," David Seville
5. "Patricia," Perez Prado

In the fall of 1958, my baby boomers left the relative security of their respective elementary schools and took a big step forward to junior-high school. The borough's junior-high school was an old building that had formerly been the high school. There was no cafeteria, and the junior-high school was dominated by a central auditorium that served not only as the gymnasium but also as a room that was used for large community meetings, concerts, assemblies, and a place for kids to gather during the lunch period to eat whatever they brought in their lunch buckets. Kids who lived close enough to the junior-high school to walk home for lunch were permitted to do so, and others could actually walk into town to occasionally eat at a restaurant for a special treat. A burger, French fries, and a Coke flavored with vanilla, chocolate, or cherry syrup cost less than one dollar, and the change was usually a sufficient tip for the waitress.

Now, there were kids from a number of elementary schools and surrounding communities at this junior-high school, not just the same ones who had spent six years together in their respective elementary schools. The time had come to make new friendships and to develop relationships that would, in many cases, last for the rest of their lives.

In seventh and eighth grades, all junior-high-school kids took the same basic classes. The kids were divided up in sections that were created based on a number of factors, including grades and possibly alphabetic listings of last names.

In ninth grade, those sections also took into account choices of potential careers for the kids. For lack of better descriptions, allow me to classify these new divisions as academic, commercial and general, including agricultural.

The academic students were those who were "smart," or who knew they probably wanted to go on to college. Those kids were the ones whose parents thought they could get loans or scholarships to pay for education beyond high school. The academic students took classes to make them more prepared for continued learning and a professional career. Role preparation by gender still took place. Boys were steered toward technical and math courses, whereas girls were prepared for careers as teachers and nurses, although a junior-high-school pigeonhole did not necessarily equate to ultimate fate in the eyes of every boy or girl.

Academic kids started learning a foreign language, and they didn't have a lot of choices. In fact, in the borough's junior-high school, only two foreign languages were offered: Latin and French. Not until high school would another, singular foreign language be offered—Spanish.

The commercial kids were those being prepared for jobs after graduating from high school. For example, girls, primarily, could get good jobs working in banks or hospitals, although a handful of boys also followed this same path. There were also business colleges and junior colleges to be considered, but most commercial kids wanted immediate employment following high-school graduation. Their curriculum included some of the academic classes mixed in with more practical classes like business math, shorthand, typing, business correspondence and bookkeeping.

A third group of kids were designated as general students. This group sometimes included agricultural and home-economics pupils—kids who might do something besides returning to their families' farms or starting a family (the latter hopefully after graduating). The general classes included some of the commercial classes and also specialized classes in cooking, sewing, metal shop, and woodshop. Some of the core classes for general students were electives for the academic and commercial students. For example, all boys had to take a semester of woodshop and a semester of metal shop, where they learned the basics, but the general students also took advanced classes in those areas. All girls took some home-economics classes, but only the general girls actually learned how to cook and sew.

There were other new experiences to be had. Among these were homerooms, gym classes, study halls, clubs, and activities, and, both shockingly and unbelievably, there were no more recesses. And possibly for the first time in my kids' lives, they realized that there were significant differences between boys and girls. Dating was on the horizon.

Kids would hurry home after school to spend time in front of their family's TV set to enjoy the burgeoning lineup of new shows. *The Mickey Mouse Club* was one of the first big-time kids' variety shows. It started in the late-1950s. The show had a regular routine including a newsreel, a cartoon, and a serial, like *Spin and Marty,* or *The Hardy Boys,* as well as musical talent and comedy segments.

For most guys, their first real love was probably Annette Funicello, one of Mousketeers on *The Mickey Mouse Club*, and for most girls, Annette's costar in several movies, Frankie Avalon, was theirs. Another of the girl's heartthrobes was Cubby O'Brien, one of the original and youngest Mousketeers.

Another TV favorite was Dick Clark's *American Bandstand*. Dick became the show's host in 1956, and, if they had older siblings, boomers sat patiently to watch the show broadcast from Philadelphia. I got to watch every show and listen to every song. As I observed my boomers watching TV, I thought almost everyone on American Bandstand was Italian and that all the Italians must have lived around Philadelphia. Back then, no one bothered to use hyphenated ethnicities, like Italian-Americans. The guy singers were all Italian; I figured that all of the girl singers were, too, except for Gogi Grant and Patti Page. I even thought the Big Bopper, Elvis, Fats Domino, and Franky Lymon and the Teenagers were Italian. The girl dancers all had huge hairdos that they kept in place with loads of hairspray, and the guy dancers were unusually well coiffed as well. All of them had "cool" clothes that you couldn't find unless you lived in a big city like Philadelphia.

A few short years later, Philadelphia actually got its own rock anthem when the nation learned that, somehow, kids who lived in Bristol were as sharp "as a pistol" (even though I didn't know pistols were sharp) because they knew how to do the Bristol Stomp. Bristol was a blue-collar suburb of Philadelphia, so obviously, to my way of thinking, you had to be Italian to live there. My boomer buddies couldn't wait to use the latest moves when they went to the Saturday-night dances at the local YMCA.

A "cool" guy at the local YMCA, who would spin 45s, seemed to get all the pretty girls' attention. The girls would all cluster in a group and show their *Bandstand* moves when the right record played. The guys would also cluster in a group on the perimeter and not ask the girls to dance for one of a few reasons: they lacked confidence, they feared rejection or, most importantly, they couldn't dance. Only the older guys knew how to dance, or thought they did, but they didn't want to get involved with a younger girl. Keep in mind, these are prepubescent youngsters who had to leave the Y at 9:00 p.m. until they reached the ripe old age of thirteen. From time to time, the guy, who was playing the records, would announce, "The next dance will be a lady's choice." I'm told that every guy in the Y would suddenly flush and watch very cautiously to see if they, or possibly a friend, might be requested by one of the girls. I'm not sure that many of the girls had any more confidence than the guys. Every so often, a girl would emerge from her crowd, walk across the basketball court to ask a guy to dance, and the rumors and teasing started almost immediately thereafter. The dance ended at 11:00 p.m., when dads would pick the kids and rush back home to watch the Gillette-sponsored fifteen-round *Fight of the Week* boxing match. If Dad allowed you to stay up, you could learn some helpful grooming tips from the Gillette commercials: "How are you fixed for blades?" and "Look sharp, feel sharp, and be sharp!" Shaving for most guys was still a while off, but any information was helpful.

It's important to talk a little about what the kids wore—or at least what the older siblings of baby boomers wore. One of the most recognizable fashion items chosen by the "in" girls was the poodle skirt. It was a long, circular felt skirt that fell anywhere from below the knee down to the ankle. These skirts often had an appliqué design on them, the most common of which was a poodle. (I'll bet you can guess where the skirt got its name.) Cutouts of records, exotic birds, flowers, and hot rods were also popular appliqués.

For a more casual look, girls often wore tucked-in, button-up blouses and sweaters. They liked Capri pants (midcalf trousers that were also called clamdiggers) in warmer weather. The shoes of choice were saddle shoes and penny loafers, so named because pennies could be inserted into the diamond-shaped slits on the shoes. My girls wore their hair in ponytails, pigtails, and bobs. It was quite popular for the girls to wear blouses that matched their tights, and for groups of girls to choose to wear the same colors on the same day. The girls loved black and white saddle shoes that they wore with bobby socks.

Boys of the fifties wore dark jeans, tight white T-shirts, and black leather jackets. Butch wax was used to keep flattops and crew cuts in place for guys with short hair. Other guys used the wax or a gel to keep their sculpted pompadours or ducktail coifs, also known as "DAs," under control. Athletes who had earned letter sweaters or letterman's jackets either wore them proudly or lent them to their girlfriends so that everyone knew whom they were dating.

My kids frequently accompanied their moms to the local grocery stores that were starting to open throughout the country. One of the gimmicks that the grocery stores and other retailers used to attract customers was a trading-stamp loyalty program. While there was competition from a number of these promotions, the absolutely largest one—and one of the the first retail-loyalty trading-stamp program—was the Sperry and Hutchison's (S&H) Green Stamp program. Other popular trading stamps included the Gold Bell Gift Stamp, the Plaid Stamp and the Blue Stamp. Although the concept had begun in the previous century, it was most popular during the 1960s.

Customers received these S&H Green Stamps and others when they purchased items at participating grocery stores, department stores, and gasoline stations, usually in increments of ten cents.

Merchants would regularly offer promotions during which they would award more stamps per dollar than their competitors, and shoppers would respond to these incentives by following the merchants with the best programs.

Kids would go home and lick and paste the stamps into books until the books were filled. Kids and their parents collected the books and ultimately exchanged them for merchandise in redemption centers at a regional Green Stamp store or via a catalog mail-in program. The stamp companies produced significantly more stamps than the US Post Office, with S&H alone issuing three times more than the post office. During the 1950s, S&H printed its own rewards catalog that became America's largest publication.

As previously mentioned, trading stamps were most popular during the 1960s. In 1965, supermarkets stopped issuing stamps and started lowering prices instead. I'm told that, even today, baby boomer think of their days spent filling books with any kind of trading stamps, as some of the most special times and memories they have.

The Leading-Edge Baby Boomers Take On High School

"And so, my fellow Americans: ask not what your country can do for you, ask what you can do for your country."
JOHN F. KENNEDY, January 20, 1961

THE YEAR 1961 STARTED ON a Sunday. In that year, notable events included the following:

* President Dwight D. Eisenhower announced that the United States had severed diplomatic and consular relations with Cuba.

* John F. Kennedy succeeded Eisenhower and became the thirty-fifth president of the United States.
* President Kennedy established the Peace Corps.
* The Bay of Pigs invasion of Cuba began, and it failed within two days.
* Both the Russians and then later the Americans put a man in space.
* President Kennedy announced the establishment of the Apollo program and his intention to put a man on the moon by the end of the decade.
* New York Yankees player Roger Maris hit his sixty-first home run, breaking the record set by Babe Ruth thirty-four years earlier.
* *Catch-22,* by Joseph Heller, was first published.
* American military involvement in Vietnam officially began, as the first American helicopters arrived in Saigon along with four hundred US personnel.

Other interesting facts include these: Federal spending was $97.72 billion, federal debt was $292.6 billion, unemployment was 5.5 percent, a first-class stamp cost $0.04, and the average price of a gallon of gasoline was $0.25.

The top Academy Awards (the thirty-fourth annual ceremony, honoring 1961 releases) were as follows:

* Best Motion Picture: *West Side Story*
* Best Actor: Maximilian Schell (*Judgment at Nuremberg*)
* Best Actress: Sophia Loren (*Two Women*)

Billboard's top-five songs of 1961 were as follows:

1. "Tossin' and Turnin'," Bobby Lewis

2. "I Fall to Pieces," Patsy Cline
3. "Michael (Row the Boat Ashore)," The Highwaymen
4. "Cryin'," Roy Orbison
5. "Runaway," Del Shannon

Finally it was time for high school and the opportunity for my boomers to demonstrate their highly advanced view of the world. Mandatory reading during the summer included J. D. Salinger's *Catcher in the Rye* and the newly published Joseph Heller book, *Catch-22*. Of course, there were other lesser-known books, including a few of my favorites, long since stored away in closets and attics, such as *The Tropic of Cancer*, which my kids read if their parents forgot to hide their copies, and other mainstays by two period authors, Max Schulman and Jack Douglas. Among Max's masterpieces were *Barefoot Boy with Cheek, Rally Round the Flag, Boys! I Was a Teenage Dwarf*, and *The Many Loves of Dobie Gillis*. Jack's contributions included *My Brother Was an Only Child, Never Trust a Naked Bus Driver*, and *A Funny Thing Happened to Me on My Way to the Grave*. I'm sure that some of my boomers' midterm goals, highly influenced by rapidly expanding TV programming, included saving enough money to buy Corvettes and drive them on *Route 66* (yes, it was both an interstate route *and* a TV program) to Hollywood, where, hopefully, they might bump into Kookie somewhere around *77 Sunset Strip* and maybe borrow his comb. My family loved watching that detective show.

High school was where kids realized that individually they were one of three types of students—students who made it happen, students who watched it happen, and students who wondered what happened. High school was also the time when it was customary to roll up your blue jeans and your short-sleeve shirts, and when the only shirts that had writing on them were worn by members of bowling teams.

Unlike junior high, where students stayed with the same group of kids all day and moved as a group for their respective subjects into different classrooms, high school was the first time where students went individually to different classes and were grouped by academic grades and test scores. In this way, they were further led in the proper, postgraduation career direction, although graduation was still three long years off. Interestingly, as I listened to the conversations among the boomers who were back for their fiftieth reunion, I could definitely pick out lasting relationships among those classmates who were part of a particular curriculum group. In fact, some of the boomers had difficulty remembering other classmates with whom they didn't attend any classes.

I won't talk about all the different classes that were available except for two special "growing-up" classes that were offered in high school. Apparently, my kids couldn't wait to take those classes.

The more urgent of the two classes was driver's education, and you had to be within a few months of turning sixteen to get scheduled for that class. Ironically, driver's education was usually taught by one of the athletic team's coaches. Why was it ironic? It was ironic because, on the one hand, the instructor was trying to coach athletes to be aggressive and to thrive on physical contact while trying at the same time, on the other hand, to teach new drivers to be calm and to avoid physical contact. Perhaps in retrospect, having the coaches teach driver's education was for rehabilitation or in retaliation for their childhood behavior. Driver's-ed. students were qualified not only to take their state licensing tests, but also to get insurance discounts.

The less urgent (but considerably more important) mandatory growing-up class was health. It was also taught by coaches. Perhaps the coaches who were selected to teach health weren't smart enough to teach driver's ed., or vice versa, or maybe the

health coaches hadn't been around long enough to have the se-
niority to teach driver's ed., or vice versa. Health class was seg-
regated by gender. Female coaches taught my baby-boomer girls,
and male coaches taught the guys. Come to think of it, very few
female coaches taught driver's education.

I'm going to share a secret. Although a house is usually a gender-
neutral, inanimate object, my story is being transcribed for me by
a male. So—with appropriate deference to the opposite gender—
the next few paragraphs will be related from a male's perspective.

According to what I've observed over the years, being a teen-
aged boy isn't all that it's cracked up to be. After all, you have to go
through puberty, a cracking voice, geekdom, and other personal
challenges. One of those challenges, or possibly opportunities, is
discovering that although boys and girls have many of the same
body parts, they also have many different parts. Apparently that
was one of the reasons behind taking health class.

Prior to health class, many of my boomer boys got their first
indications of those gender differences from *National Geographic*,

especially those editions that featured photographs of primitive cultures that generally lived in the jungles and rainforests of, for example, South America or Africa. Absolutely nothing can capture a prepubescent boy's attention quicker than a topless Ubangi woman washing her clothes in a tributary of the Congo River in Central Africa.

But now, all the boys in the health class were going to be taught something they instinctively suspected, although not all of my boys had the exact same suspicion at exactly the same time. This absolutely crucial instruction was taught by a coach, who might possibly not have manifested the most profound characteristics of sensitivity and compassion.

It was time for my boys to have formal education about human sexuality and reproduction. There were actually technical words for the body parts that my boys knew they had but for which they used more ribald terms. There were also body parts that my boys probably weren't aware even existed and were actually hidden somewhere in or on their bodies. The coach, now also known as the health teacher, wrote these words on the blackboard, and he even had pictures and diagrams of them: "puberty," "scrotum," "testicles," "vas deferens," and "epididymis."

But what about the thing every boy wanted and needed to know? We were getting there, right after the health teacher let the boys know that one testicle always hung lower than the other one (I think he said it was always the left one, but I must confess to not having firsthand knowledge) so that a boy can comfortably cross his legs. Wasn't our creator thoughtful?

And then came the pièce de résistance, the bottom line. He told my boys two things. Number one was something to the effect that when you're with a member of the opposite sex and you take off your clothes, you're really naked! That begs the question:

What? Are you naked in the physical sense, naked in the moral sense, and/or naked in the psychological sense? Did that mean you actually had to undress to have sex? The kids got no explanation! But let's move on quickly to point number two.

Number two was equally puzzling. The health teacher suggested that it was best to not become sexually intimate (whatever that meant) with one of your classmates (probably of the opposite gender) because you might eventually meet up with that classmate again at a class reunion, and it could be embarrassing. I can't help but wonder how many of my visitors needed to recall that lesson during their fiftieth reunion. And that was the end of health class!

A few of these boomers apparently understood what the health teacher was talking about. There were quite a few of them who were not only celebrating their fiftieth high-school reunion but also their fiftieth wedding anniversaries nearly at the same time. They also had children who were nearing age fifty. I often wondered why some classmates suddenly dropped out of school so close to graduation. Finally, I learned the answer.

Having successfully absorbed those lessons, my baby boomers were nearing that time when driver's ed. finally bore fruit, and they actually started to drive. In my opinion, cars that baby boomers either had in their families, drove, or wanted to own are among the things that elicit the most definite memories from them, at least from the males. The other thing is the music to which they listened, sang, or danced, and that memory, for sure, is not gender-specific.

"Rocket 88," by Jackie Brenston

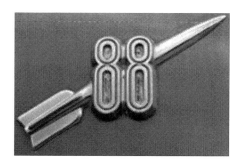

FOLLOWING THE END OF WORLD War II, American manufacturing switched from producing war-related items to making consumer goods. Automobiles certainly met a need, and, at the start of the 1960s, nearly 17 percent of working Americans had jobs related to the automotive industry. They were building and selling classic, powerful vehicles that had style but were the most unsafe cars ever manufactured. Hard-top convertibles were developed early in the fifties, followed by optional air conditioning in 1951 and then power steering.

Early in the 1960s, Detroit and its Big Three automakers made cars for a couple of different consumer needs. Some drivers wanted smaller, fuel-efficient vehicles, but others in the driving public wanted more power. As the decade progressed, the two segments actually came together with midsize muscle cars, the first of which was the Pontiac GTO. Muscle cars became the rage. The first economy cars included GM's Buick Special, Oldsmobile F-85, and Pontiac Tempest. Chevrolet offered the Corvair and its sporty sibling, the Monza. Chrysler brought the Dodge Dart and the Plymouth Valiant to the market, and Ford's Falcon, with its Futura upgrade, was the Blue Oval's entry. In 1964, the first graduation year for my boomers, Ford pioneered its new model, the Mustang, and that car was featured extensively at the New York World's Fair. The fair included a conveyor belt ride where visitors actually rode in real Ford convertibles. General Motors responded quickly with its introduction of the Chevrolet Camaro, the Chevy Super Sport or "SS" models, and the Pontiac Firebird.

Many of these new cars came with very few options, and frequently radios, seat belts, and backup lights had to be installed by mechanics after they were purchased at stores like Western Auto and Pep Boys. Many of these cars also came with manual transmissions and three-speed column, or "four-on-the-floor" shift mechanisms. Tires with white walls were made of soft rubber, and that tire composition permitted a very macho teenage behavior: "laying rubber." That behavior also resulted in a lot of clutch, brakes and tire replacements, and quite a few traffic tickets as well.

Some kids actually owned their own cars instead of having to drive their parent's cars (if and when they were lucky enough to be allowed to take the family car). The kids with their own cars were always looking to customize them to make them distinct and appealing. They changed the car's original carburetors to "six-packs," which were three two-barrel carburetors, or to dual "quads," meaning two four-barrel carburetors. They stroked and bored the engine blocks and "huffed" the power by adding turbos or superchargers. Then, they'd "chop and channel" the cars' bodies, "French" the lights and antennas, "tube" the rear wheel openings, and add larger tires and wheels.

These gearheads frequently hung things, like dice, on the rear view mirror, and put "suicide" knobs on their steering wheels. These steering wheel items, also known as "brodie" or "necker" knobs, were theoretically designed to make steering with one hand easier. Most cars of this time didn't have power steering, and letting go of the knob after completing a turn could result in the knob hitting the driver's arm and creating some serious pain. The reference to a "necker" knob meant that a male driver, for example, who could now steer with one arm, could put his other arm around his girlfriend, who sat next to him. Because most cars also lacked seat belts, she could easily slide over and sit in the middle of the seat.

During the 1960s, new car models were always introduced in the fall, usually on a specific day before which the public wasn't allowed to see them. The new cars were covered with material so that no one could see them while they were being delivered to the various dealerships on car haulers. The dealerships covered their windows with paper or opaque, paint-like material until the day of the grand opening. Visiting a dealership's showroom on intro day was a social highlight each year.

In the sixties and probably long thereafter, Detroit implemented a hierarchy of models that it developed to meet the demographics of its customers. In other words, the industry accorded status by car brand. Entry-level vehicles were typical among the blue-collar families and generally included Fords, Chevys, or Plymouths. Midlevel vehicles were those belonging to the middle-class community: Mercurys, Dodges, and Pontiacs. The wealthy families drove Oldsmobiles, Buicks, Chryslers, Lincolns, and Cadillacs.

"I Get Around," by the Beach Boys

———— ❧ ————

AFTER MY BOOMER BUDDIES GOT their licenses and had access to cars, they participated in a social activity called cruising. Cruising probably had started in East Los Angeles, where "low-riders" started having fun during the 1940s and spread throughout the rest of the country via Detroit and a few other cities until it finally reached my borough and other small towns throughout the US. Cruising has been characterized as "social and recreational driving on an impulsively random, often aimless course." My baby boomers, who were attending the fiftieth reunion, frequently had participated in cruising in towns around the area, where they rode with their friends, usually of the same gender, with the hopes of passing, waving to, and possibly even meeting other cruisers of the opposite gender. I'm not saying there wasn't much to do in the sixties because that's not true, but cruising was one of the "in" things.

Cruising and eating frozen custard and pizza went together. Inevitably, the cruisers would wind up in a restaurant to have real meals, like burgers, fries, and flavored Cokes or milkshakes. Working boomers got paid about $1.50 an hour, and the aforementioned meal would cost about $1.00. Songs in a jukebox cost a nickel a play, or six plays for a quarter, and a great tip for your waitress was anything from a quarter to fifty cents. Money seemed to go a long way.

Suddenly, going to the local YMCA for the Saturday-night dance wasn't sufficient, especially after boomers learned that neighboring communities, fire halls, clubs, and amusement parks also had dances. Now that my kids were mobile, going to a neighboring community meant they could meet and socialize with other kids with whom they hadn't grown up. A change of scenery was appealing.

There were a number of excellent amusement parks within an hour or two, and they became destinations of choice. In addition to the rides, both thrill-seeking and romantic, there were swimming pools, bingo parlors, band stands, dance halls, the most delicious junk food stands and penny arcades with their games of skill (or luck). Almost none of the games in the penny arcade cost a penny, but they were alluring and colorful machines which my boomers couldn't avoid. Urban expansion for commercial and housing developments has unfortunately resulted in the subsequent closure of many of these glorious parks.

Another place you could go if you had a car was to a drive-in movie. The drive-in boom in America was in full swing during the 1950s, with growth from around one thousand theaters in the late 1940s to more than five thousand by the end of the 1950s. Coincidentally the number of indoor theaters declined by nearly that same number during that same period. A few drive-ins even opened near my borough. The largest drive-ins, which were located in Michigan and Texas, had room for three thousand cars, and the smallest ones had room for only fifty cars.

Drive-ins, theoretically, were built for drivers to take their entire families to the movies, to park near posts on which speakers were located and to mount the speakers on the drivers' windows. The drive-ins had a concession area where popcorn and other, primarily junk food, could be purchased. In fact, the movies had an actual intermission so that the audience could walk to the concession area to spend some money. A popular game was to hide friends in the car's trunk so that they didn't have to pay to enter the theater. Many of my boomers went to drive-in theaters with dates to practice what they had been told not to do during their respective health classes. That's enough about drive-in movie theaters. I'll leave the rest to your imagination.

"Itsy Bitsy Teenie Weenie Yellow Polka Dot Bikini," by Brian Hyland

⸰⸰⸰

"Itsy bitsy teenie weenie yellow Polka Dot Bikini" was a story of a young girl who had gone to a locker room and changed into her bikini, but is too scared to come out of that room. Eventually, she makes it to the beach, but sits wrapped up in her blanket. Finally, she gets into the water, where she stays, despite getting very cold, because she's too afraid to come out and go back to the beach. The "new" swimsuit, which had actually been invented in 1946, was seen by some as too risqué for the mainstream. But the Hyland song is widely credited for resulting in a rapid increase in the sale of bikinis and for helping them to become accepted in society.

Support for the bikini's popularity came from Hollywood, too. Two movies in the first half of the 1960s created iconic moments in both cinematic and fashion history, to my mind. In 1962, Ursula Andress appeared in the James Bond film *Dr. No*; she rose out of the Caribbean in a white bikini with a large diving knife on her hip. In 1964, in *Bikini Beach*, everyone's favorite former Mousketeer, Annette Funicello, appeared in a number of scenes along the California coast wearing a bikini. She had finally been permitted to trade in the standard, two-piece bathing suits that she had worn in other "beach party" movies of the era. Until then, the bikini was seen by some as being too risqué for the mainstream.

Fashion in the sixties was different from that of the preceding decade. Many thought that girls' clothes were starting to look more "masculine" and boys' clothes were becoming more "feminine"-looking. The flared trousers known as bell bottoms, already part of a US sailor's Navy uniform, exemplified this trend; they became almost as popular as jeans. "Unisex" clothing would eventually find its place in the fashion world of the times, too.

Time Out for an Anachronism

—∞∞∞—

I'M GOING TO STEP OUT of the time period of this book for a moment. If you live around one of America's entertainment cities, like Nashville, Las Vegas, or other cosmopolitan centers, you have a great opportunity to experience live performances of many types because lots of entertainers come to those cities. If you purchase a high-cost ticket, you can go see touring A-listers, and there are lots of them. Younger folks can have those entertainers all to themselves.

The *real* entertainers are the ones who are still performing in smaller venues like they did when leading-edge baby boomers graduated from high school. They are groups like the Lettermen, the Kingston Trio, the Four Freshmen, the Drifters, the Coasters, Herman's Hermits, and the Turtles—you know who I mean. Individuals like Frankie Avalon, Debbie Reynolds, and others who also still perform.

When you go to one of these shows, you'll quickly notice that, based on how they respond to the performers, it looks like nearly all the baby boomers in the audience shared the original experiences. The music they danced to (or watched the "cool kids" dance to) on Saturday nights at the YMCA, the volunteer-fire hall, the amusement park, or, occasionally, at the high school wasn't exclusive to kids from central Pennsylvania. This comes as no surprise, I'm sure. You can see the enjoyment all around at outdoor concerts wherever they might be held. How do all these old codgers know that music? Why do they all sing along, and how do they all know all the words? The answer is simple: Inside the body of every leading-edge baby boomer, in fact every baby boomer as well, is a young person wondering what the heck happened. I've heard it said that, "growing old is mandatory, but growing up is optional." In other words, "you can't help getting older, but you don't have to get old." Enough said … let's move on!

"Rock around the Clock," by Bill Haley & His Comets

———— ∽⃝⃝⃝ ————

ALLOW ME TO RETURN TO the appropriate time period and speak about the music of the 1950s and 1960s. Although lots of things were peculiar to baby boomers, especially those who were teenagers during that decade, music was possibly the cement that held this generation together, not only during those times, but also for years—no, *decades*—thereafter.

Two films that were released about ten years after the baby-boom period had officially ended, *American Graffiti* and its sequel, *More American Graffiti*, were able to document (as well as any media ever did) the music and activities, like cruising and drive-in movie-going, of the period. Set in 1962 Modesto, California, the movies were about my boomers, regardless of where they grew up or lived. The movies waxed nostalgic about teenage life in the 1960s, and their soundtracks were incredible. Watching those "flicks" was like watching *American Bandstand*, but without Dick Clark, and all the boomers who saw the movies certainly knew all the lyrics to all the songs.

OK, by now you know that I like to give a bit of historical background on the way I see things, so here's another "blast from the past," which is appropriate because that's how a typical rock 'n' roll song, a piece of my boomers' music, is frequently described.

I don't want to go back as far as I can (remember, I was a teenager about 150 years ago), so let's start just about ten years before my visitors were born, say the mid-1930s. At that time, popular music was in transition from the jazz of the previous decade to a new form of jazz, called "swing." Very large bands, that is, "big bands," sprang up all over America and played swing arrangements with either a Kansas City or a New York flavor. My favorite bandleaders were Glenn Miller, Benny Goodman, Tommy and Jimmy Dorsey, Count Basie, and Duke Ellington, just to name a few. Their music could be heard everywhere, and the bands were constantly on the road, playing one-night or longer stands in cities both large and small all over America.

Swing had its own culture, including its own dances, cloth-ing style, and slang expressions like "jive talk," "hep," "hootchy cootchy," "hoofer," "the cat's meow," "hi-de-ho," "swanky," "spiffy," and "scram." Swing dancing of the 1930s became jitterbugging, and the coolest "hepsters" dressed in their finest "zoot suits" grabbed their best "mop" and jitterbugged their improvised "breakouts" and "aerial moves"; they often became a part of the show. Swing culture was a youthful alternative to the conventions and restric-tions of middle-class life.

Then came World War II, with its need for Americans to support the war effort in many ways, including rationing and restrictions on petroleum products and other consumer items. The hepsters be-came soldiers and sailors, and their mops worked in factories. Swing gave way to what was called "bebop" or simply "bop"; new bands, led by the likes of Dizzy Gillespie and Charlie Parker, emerged. Big bands had to tour in order to support their overheads, and the limi-tations on gasoline and tires made those tours harder to sustain. The big bands evolved into smaller groups that were more in tune with changing popular dances, and these smaller groups became "jump" and "rhythm-and-blues," a.k.a. "R-and-B" acts.

So, my friends, the baby boomers were starting to come of age in the early 1950s as the big-band era drew to a close, but the American pop charts were still dominated by songs performed by those bands' singers, namely Frank Sinatra, Doris Day, Nat King Cole, Rosemary Clooney, and Frankie Laine. Into this mix entered Alan Freed, a disc jockey who in 1951 played black R-and-B records at his station, WJW Cleveland, and described them with the term "rock 'n' roll."

As the 1950s wore on, rock 'n' roll became segmented into sev-eral genres, including rhythm and blues, pop, folk revival, doo-wop, rockabilly, teen idols, and jazz. Examples of each include, but are not limited to, the following:

+ Rhythm and blues: Little Richard, the Platters, Bo Diddley
+ Pop: Doris Day, Johnny Mathis, Tony Bennett, the Four Aces
+ Folk revival: Pete Seeger, the Kingston Trio, Harry Belafonte
+ Doo-wop: Frankie Lymon and the Teenagers, the Diamonds
+ Rockabilly: Elvis Presley, Johnny Cash, Bill Haley & His Comets
+ Teen idols: Ricky Nelson, Frankie Avalon, Annette Funicello
+ Jazz: Miles Davis, Sarah Vaughn, Louis Armstrong

The ability to record music and hear it played on the radio made the live performances of touring big bands even less popular. Technology improvements also made record players more affordable; now people could play what they wanted to hear when they wanted to hear it. The 78-rpm record had been replaced by the LP (long-playing) vinyl album, and, in about 1949, the 45-rpm single had been introduced.

Records were generally sold in record stores, and I'm not being cute or redundant when I say that. Consumers had limited choices of record formats: 78s, 45s, and 33s or LPs, as mentioned earlier. The number referred to how many times a record player's turntable revolved each minute. A 78 was customarily ten inches in diameter and held about three minutes of music; there were also twelve-inch versions that could hold up to five minutes of music. They were made out of some kind of material that shattered easily, and they were on their way out in the late 1950s.

The 78s started to disappear as the more modern LPs became popular. These newer records rotated about 40 percent as fast as their predecessors, and they were made out of vinyl. They were about twelve inches in diameter and sometimes had tracks that permitted multiple songs to be played on each side of the record. Almost concurrent with the advent of rock 'n' roll, the music of my baby boomers, the 45 record appeared in a seven-inch format with a big hole in the middle instead of the smaller hole used by both its earlier formats. You needed to have an adapter if you wanted to play a 45 on a traditional record player if, and only if, that particular record player also had a 45-rpm setting on it. The newer 45s didn't last long, relatively speaking, as various bands, most notably the Beatles, started to bring out "concept albums." These LP concept albums had all the music related to a single unified theme or unified story. On the other hand, the 45 generally had one song on the front (the A side) and another on the reverse (the B side or flip side), whereas an LP album could hold ten to twelve songs. An occasional 45 would even have hits on both the A and the B sides. By the end of the 1960s, the 45 had all but disappeared, at least in the United States.

In 1955, rock 'n' roll had its first chart-topper with Bill Haley & His Comets' "Rock around the Clock." In April 1956, Elvis Presley, who had started his music career at age nineteen in 1954, topped the charts with "Heartbreak Hotel," and by the end of that same year, he would be the first artist ever to have nine singles in the top 100 at one time. By the end of the decade, in 1959, rock 'n' roll records would account for 43 percent of all records sold. Some rock 'n' roll historians suggest that the initial phase of rock 'n' roll came to an end in 1959 following the retirement of Little Richard to become a preacher in 1957, the scandal surrounding Jerry Lee Lewis's marriage to his thirteen-year-old cousin in 1958, Elvis's entering the army in 1958, and the deaths of Buddy Holly, Ritchie Valens, and the Big Bopper in a plane crash, the arrest of Chuck Berry, and the breaking of the Payola scandal, all in 1959. One of my boomer's good friends, who has chronicled the history of rock and roll from its start in the early 1950's, claims the music actually died in 1993. That's when the combined sales of country and western music and rap recordings exceed the sales of rock and roll recordings.

In the sixties, AM radio was the rage; FM radio was still limited in both the number of stations that were available and the distance that an FM radio signal could travel. The best rock 'n' roll music was played by a few great AM radio stations that rural baby boomers couldn't hear until the evening because of reception issues, including interference from the aurora borealis. A number of power radio stations surrounded our borough, relatively speaking, and at night my boomers were treated to programs from WABC in New York City, WBZ in Boston, WKBW in Buffalo, New York, and WIBG in Philadelphia.

Certain disc jockeys, also known as "DJs" or "deejays" became larger than life, almost pop-culture stars. Along with Alan Freed, the disc jockey from Cleveland who is widely credited with coining the term "rock 'n' roll," there were two New York City guys, "Murray the K" Kaufman and "Cousin Brucie" Morrow (who would later become a staple of satellite radio); Wolfman Jack, who broadcast on the West Coast from a pirate radio station in Mexico; Casey Kasem and "The Real" Don Steele, from Los Angeles; Dick Biondi, from Chicago; and Arnie "Woo Woo" Ginsberg, from the Boston area.

These DJs were responsible for creating hit records and hit performers by repeatedly playing their music on their respective stations.

Just as the prior generation had its dances, so did the baby boomers. In the '60s, it was fun to collect, share and trade 45 records that cost less than a dollar. So, driven by the latest fad(s), able to buy lots of 45s, and willing to exhibit somewhat silly behavior in public, the boomers became choreographers. Some recording artists and record labels actually released records to start a new dance fad. There were also printed instructions so baby boomer parents could imitate the behavior. How horrifying must have it been to actually see a boomer parent behaving like a teenager?

How many of these dances can you remember?

* The Twist
* The Stroll
* The Hand Jive
* The Jitterbug
* The Mashed Potato
* The Monster Mash
* The Hully Gully
* The Freddie

* The Swim
* The Bristol Stomp

How many of them can you still do? Be careful, though ... you're now a grown up.

"The Navy Hymn," by William Whiting

PROBABLY THE ONE, MOST PROFOUND thing that leading-edge boomers still can recall happened during their senior year. All of my buddies, except for those few who might have been ill and absent from classes on Friday, November 22, 1963, near the end of the school day, remember what class they were in when their principal announced on the high school's public-address system that President John F. Kennedy had been assassinated in Dallas.

> Eternal Father, strong to save,
> Whose arm hath bound the restless wave,
> Who bidd'st the mighty ocean deep
> Its own appointed limits keep;
> Oh, hear us when we cry to Thee,
> For those in peril on the sea!

The death of Kennedy, our president and a decorated naval officer in World War II, was riveting. The eagerly anticipated weekend before Thanksgiving became especially somber with all the television coverage devoted to what had just happened.

Lee Harvey Oswald, the alleged shooter was captured on Saturday, November 23. On Sunday, November 24, as Oswald was being moved to a more secure jail, an enraged civilian, Jack Ruby, emerged from the crowd of onlookers and fatally shot Oswald.

President Kennedy was buried on Monday, November 25. The image of his young son, "John-John," saluting his father was indelibly imprinted on almost everyone's mind.

The days of American Camelot were over. Three days after the funeral, on Thursday, November 28, a very somber Thanksgiving was celebrated. And then, it was time to get ready for the holidays.

"Graduation Day," by
the Four Freshmen

*"Let us carry forward the plans and the programs of John
Fitzgerald Kennedy ---not because of sorrow or sympathy,
but because they are right."*
LYNDON BAINES JOHNSON, January 8, 1964

JANUARY 1, 1964 WAS A Wednesday, and it kicked off another leap
year. On the surface for most Americans, life seemed pretty simple.
In general, teachers didn't say much about diversity and racism.
Gender had a huge influence on possible career aspirations, and
professionals knew that they had to "earn their stripes" in order
to advance in the workplace. But this was to be a year of political
awakening.

During that year, notable events included the following:

- *Introducing the Beatles* was released by Chicago's Vee-Jay Records to get the jump on Capitol Records's release of *Meet the Beatles!* The latter was scheduled for release ten days later. The two companies fought over this issue in court.
- The US surgeon general reported that smoking could be hazardous to one's health (the first such statement from the US government).
- Plans to build the World Trade Center were announced.
- The Beatles appeared on the Ed Sullivan Show.
- Cassius Clay beat Sonny Liston to become the heavyweight champion of the world. Clay later changed his name to Muhammad Ali and announced that he had joined the Nation of Islam.
- The first Ford Mustang rolled off the assembly line.
- A Dallas jury found Jack Ruby guilty of killing John F. Kennedy's assassin, Lee Harvey Oswald.
- The Rolling Stones released their debut album, *The Rolling Stones.*
- The 1964 New York World's Fair opened.
- Three civil-rights workers were murdered near Philadelphia, Mississippi, by local Ku Klux Klansmen and a deputy sheriff.
- The United States sent five thousand more military advisors to South Vietnam, bringing the total number of US forces in Vietnam to twenty-one thousand. Subsequent events led the US Congress to pass the Gulf of Tonkin resolution, which effectively started the Vietnam War.
- Dr. Martin Luther King, Jr., age thirty-five, was awarded the Nobel Peace Prize for his nonviolent civil-rights activism. At the time, he was the youngest person to ever receive the prize.

Also interesting were the facts that federal spending was $118.53 billion, federal debt was $316.1 billion, unemployment was 5.7 percent, a first-class stamp cost $0.05, and the average price of a gallon of gasoline was $0.30.

The top Academy Awards (the thirty-seventh annual ceremony, honoring 1964 releases) were as follows:

  ❋ Best Motion Picture: *My Fair Lady*
  ❋ Best Actor: Rex Harrison (*My Fair Lady*)
  ❋ Best Actress: Julie Andrews (*Mary Poppins*)

Billboard's top-five songs of 1964 were as follows:

1. "I Want to Hold Your Hand," the Beatles
2. "She Loves You," the Beatles
3. "Hello, Dolly," Louis Armstrong
4. "Oh, Pretty Woman," Roy Orbison
5. "I Get Around," the Beach Boys

In addition to the aforementioned notable events, shortly after the start of the year, conservative Republican Arizona senator Barry Goldwater announced his candidacy for president of the United States, seeking his party's nomination to run against President Lyndon Johnson, who had assumed that position after the assassination of John F. Kennedy less than two months before. In November, Johnson won a landslide victory with more than 60 percent of the popular vote.

In February, *The Feminine Mystique* by Betty Friedan was released as a paperback, and the book's sales in its first printing totaled more than 1.4 million copies. The "mystique" she wrote about was "the idea that women were naturally fulfilled by devoting their lives to being housewives and mothers." Housewives across America began to express dissatisfaction with their domestic roles, and a transformative feminist movement began to deal with the "problem with no name." Friedan became the first president of the National Organization for Women, and wrote, "We can no longer ignore the voice within women that says: 'I want something more than my husband and my children and my home.'"

In April, at the 36th Annual Academy Awards (honoring 1963 releases), actor Sidney Poitier became the first black man to win a Best Actor Oscar for his role in *Lilies of the Field*. As he accepted his award, he took a deep breath and said, "It has been a long journey to this moment."

A few months later, in June, a black man in South Africa, Nelson Mandela, was convicted of sabotage and sentenced to life in prison.

"Soldier Boy," by the Shirelles

THIS 1962 HIT CERTAINLY WAS prescient for my boys in that it spoke about wherever those boys might go, no matter what port or foreign shore. In June, leading-edge baby boomers throughout the entire country begin to graduate from high school, and the eighteen-year-old boys who were graduating registered for the draft as required by the Selective Training and Service Act of 1940. The draft allowed the armed forces to fill military vacancies that could not be filled through voluntary means. The boys were identified with a number and a letter that showed their status with respect to potential service. The most common of these classifications were as follows:

SELECTIVE SERVICE SYSTEM

ORDER TO REPORT FOR INDUCTION

Approval Not Required.

The President of the United States,

To

(Local Board Stamp)

August 11th, 1965
(Date of mailing)

SELECTIVE SERVICE NO.

GREETING:

You are hereby ordered for induction into the Armed Forces of the United States, and to report at ARMED FORCES EXAMINING & INDUCTION STATION - 2ND FLOOR, BLDG. 13, 1519 ALASKAN WAY SOUTH, SEATTLE 4, WASHINGTON

on September 7th, 1965 at 8:00 A. M.

for forwarding to an Armed Forces Induction Station.

* **1-A**: Available for military service
* **1-D**: Member of reserve component or student taking military training
* **2-A**: Registrant deferred because of civilian occupation
* **2-S**: Registrant deferred because of activity in study
* **3-A**: Registrant with a child or children; registrant deferred by reason of extreme hardship to dependents
* **4-F**: Registrant not qualified for any military service

In August, the USS *Maddox* (DD-731) fired warning shots over three attacking North Vietnamese torpedo boats. Two days later, the USS *Turner Joy* (DD-951) joined in the patrols and reported, possibly falsely, another attack by North Vietnamese torpedo boats in what would become known as the Gulf of Tonkin

Incident. Orders were issued for American airplanes to bomb North Vietnam.

Between the years 1956 and 1963, American military deaths in the Vietnam Conflict had totaled 200. During 1964 alone, 216 more Americans died in that conflict. My baby boomers who graduated during that summer and either volunteered or were drafted into military service completed their basic training later that year, and many were sent to Vietnam as part of the American buildup. The year after, in 1965, American deaths increased ninefold to nearly two thousand, and, through the remainder of the decade, more than forty-six thousand American military personnel were killed. Their civilian peers who remained at home were actively lobbying against the country's involvement in the conflict. When my boomers returned home from duty overseas, they did not get the heroes' welcomes afforded to their dads as they returned from World War II and Korea. Parades had been replaced with protests.

*"Sooner or later, all the people of the world will have to
discover a way to live together in peace."*
MARTIN LUTHER KING, December 10, 1964

"The Times They Are a Changin'," by Bob Dylan

IT WAS A CALL FOR people, writers, critics, senators, congressmen, mothers and fathers to realize that their sons and daughters had moved on.

At the same time, civil-rights activism was spreading fast; it wouldn't be long before any efforts by teachers to keep on avoiding the subject of racism would be disallowed. From the middle to the end of June, about one thousand out-of-state volunteers participated in one of two one-week orientation sessions held at Western College for Women in Oxford, Ohio. These volunteers, most of whom were young, from the North, and predominantly white, participated alongside thousands of black Mississippians in Freedom Summer. The Mississippi voting procedure at the time required blacks to fill out a twenty-one-question registration form and to answer, to the satisfaction of the white registrar, a question on interpretation of any one of 285 sections of the state constitution.

On or about June 21 or 22, 1964, one day after the first group of Freedom Summer volunteers arrived in Mississippi, three civil-rights workers, Michael Schwerner, Andrew Goodman, and James Chaney, set out to investigate a church bombing near Philadelphia, Mississippi. The three activists were arrested for a traffic violation and held for several hours. When they were released at 10:30 p.m., it was the last time they were seen alive. Their bodies would not be found until early August.

Fred Arnow

While the three civil-rights workers were still missing, President Johnson signed the Civil Rights Act of 1964 into law. The act prohibited discrimination on the basis of race, color, religion, sex, or national origin in employment, ended segregation in public places, and outlawed segregation practices common among many southern businesses for decades. In December, the US Justice Department charged twenty-one Mississippi men with conspiracy to deny civil rights (murder is not a federal crime). Seven were found guilty, although none of them would spend more than six years in jail.

In the fall, student activists at the University of California—Berkeley, many of whom had participated in Freedom Summer, distributed information on racial discrimination at a row of tables set up at the corner of Bancroft and Telegraph Streets, a location that had traditionally been a place to share information about a variety of campus activities and events. Berkeley administrators told the students they must keep all political activities off campus. Students saw this as a violation of their First Amendment rights and began a protest that lasted for two days, involved thousands of students, and resulted in more than eight hundred arrests. Student demonstrations at Berkeley continued throughout the fall semester, inspired similar protests across the country, and helped define modern American student activism.

Toward the end of summer, the Supremes topped the *Billboard* charts, joining fellow black performers such as James Brown and Marvin Gaye in the racial integration of popular music. Their label, Motown Records, released music that appealed to audiences of all races and enabled black artists to cross over into the pop charts.

It had been almost impossible to see a concert where black and white artists shared the same stage. However, in October, a show in Santa Monica, California, the Teenage Awards Music

International (TAMI), ignored the racial biases of the era and included the Supremes and James Brown alongside the Beach Boys and the Rolling Stones, along with other performers who crossed the racial divide.

In addition to the aforementioned top-five *Billboard* hits for 1964, the popularity of the next fifteen hit songs illustrates how eagerly my singing and dancing baby boomers accepted a variety of performers, regardless of race, gender or nationality:

6. "Everybody Loves Somebody," Dean Martin
7. "My Guy," Mary Wells
8. "We'll Sing in the Sunshine," Gale Garnett
9. "Last Kiss," J. Frank Wilson and the Cavaliers
10. "Where Did Our Love Go?" The Supremes
11. "People," Barbra Streisand
12. "Java," Al Hirt
13. "A Hard Day's Night," The Beatles
14. "Love Me Do," The Beatles
15. "Do Wah Diddy Diddy," Manfred Mann
16. "Please Please Me," The Beatles
17. "Dancing in the Street," Martha and the Vandellas
18. "Little Children," Billy J. Kramer and the Dakotas
19. "Love Me with All of Your Heart," Ray Charles
20. "Under the Boardwalk," The Drifters

The year 1964 ended on a Thursday. The Dow Jones Industrial Average closed at 874, up 112 points or nearly 13 percent from its closing a year earlier. The average cost of a new house was $13,500, the average cost of a new car was $3,500, and average annual income was $6,000. The major, post–World War II shortages in jobs, housing, and food had ended.

When my baby boomers had arrived on earth only eighteen years earlier, the average cost of a new house had been only $5,600, the average cost of a new car had been $1,120, and an average annual income was $2,500. In those eighteen years, the cost of housing had increased about 150 percent, a car's price had gone up by nearly 200 percent, and wages had kept pace, increasing about 140 percent. Relatively speaking, big-ticket items were still quite affordable.

In 1964, futurist Alvin Toffler, in acknowledging the earlier work of Betty Friedan's book, declared that the trigger on history had been pulled.

"It's a Small World," by the Sherman Brothers

POSSIBLY THE MOST PERFORMED AND most widely translated single on earth, "It's a Small World" was written in the wake of the Cuban Missile Crisis and was never copyrighted at the request of UNICEF (UN International Children's Fund), which the song saluted. The song speaks to one moon, one golden sun, and a smile meaning friendship to everyone. It talks about a "world of laughter" and a "world of tears." It also speaks to "a world of hopes and a world of fears."

"It's a Small World," like my baby boomers, also celebrated its fiftieth anniversary in 2014. The public first heard the infectious theme song on April 22, 1964, the opening day of the 1964 New York World's Fair.

Lawrence R. Samuel referred to that World's Fair as *The End of the Innocence*, in his scholarly account of the expo. Notes on the book provide the following background:

On the eve of the opening day, a twelve billion-candlepower beam of light was turned on over the fairgrounds, visible from New Haven, Connecticut, to Atlantic City, New Jersey, and outshining Times Square. Soon, the world's largest fountain would be turned on and a 610-bell carillon would ring out, "There's No Business Like Show Business." Already a highly contentious political battleground and social phenomenon, "the single greatest event in history" was finally about to begin.

From April to October in 1964 and 1965, some 52 million people from around the world flocked to the New York World's Fair, an experience that lives on in the memory of many individuals and in America's collective consciousness. Lawrence R. Samuel offers a thought-provoking portrait of this seminal event and of the cultural climate that surrounded it, countering critics' assessment of the Fair as the "ugly duckling" of global expositions. Opening just five months after President Kennedy's assassination, the Fair allowed millions to celebrate international brotherhood while the conflict in Vietnam came to a boil. The Fair glorified the postwar American dream of limitless optimism, just as a counterculture of sex, drugs, and rock 'n' roll was coming into being.

It was, in short, the last gasp of the American Dream.

"It's a small world after all," as the simple atmosphere enjoyed by the boomers seemed over along with the boom itself.

Epilogue: "Will You Love Me Tomorrow," by the Shirelles

———⟨⟨⟨———

THE "GOLDEN" REUNION OF THE members of the class of 1964, who had graduated from the high school named for the small town fifty years earlier, was over.

Following the pleasant Thursday-night gathering for pizza night with me, the House on Pine Street, my buddies enjoyed two subsequent evenings together. Friday night's event was for classmates only. They met in a local establishment for nearly five hours to reconnect and remember. Some of them had maintained their friendships since graduating, and others jumped right in and started to discuss memories and stories of years gone by. People who are sixty-eight do not have the endurance of those who are eighteen, and the night ended happily and safely and early.

Saturday was the night for spouses, friends, and guests to accompany the classmates to a more formal evening with a cocktail hour and a sit-down dinner. The event's organizers had planned an organized program with an open microphone so that anyone who wanted to speak could have an opportunity. The class officers were presented, a slideshow that memorialized photographs of my kids from childhood to present was shown, and both formal and informal comments were delivered. I was especially proud when my owner was presented with a bouquet in appreciation for her sharing me with my friends during the pizza nights. I'm still glowing from that recognition.

My kids who had passed away were appropriately recognized, and acknowledgments were made to the couples who had been married fifty years. It was heartwarming to see that many of those relationships had actually thrived, despite the lack of meaningful instruction in health class. The class's military veterans were accorded tributes that might have been denied years earlier when they left military service amid antiwar protests. One classmate's spouse, a highly decorated Vietnam veteran, spontaneously rose to acknowledge his wife and the wives of all the veterans. The evening ended, of course, but the night still lives on in so many ways. And so does pizza night, with a smaller group visiting me on a recurring basis.

In the title song of this epilogue, the Shirelles and other singers like Carole King (who cowrote the song) and Roberta Flack asked how much time they could expect to share with the objects of their affections, and these words rang so true for my friends with regard to their classmates. Since the reunion, several more classmates have passed away, and a few have had serious medical episodes. As time passes, a question lingers: Should my large group of friends wait another five years to reconvene in their hometown, or should they get together sooner? I know a committed few will always meet periodically as long as my owner and I are there to welcome them, but how many of the others will?

If I were a betting object, I'd put my money on the classmates meeting again for the same types of events in only two years this time, when the leading-edge baby boomers are turning seventy. And if my story is well accepted among its readers, I hope to continue this saga with a sequel that might end when the trailing-edge baby boomers, those born in 1964, graduated from high school in 1982. I can tell you from firsthand knowledge that those subsequent eighteen years were quite different from the eighteen years I've tried to describe in this book.

And thus, the journey is either ending or just beginning. It all depends on how you answer the age-old question: Is the glass half full, or is it half empty? My answer to that is: It all depends on whether you're pouring or drinking!

"Let me bring you up to speed … we know nothing.
You are now up to speed."
INSPECTOR JACQUES CLOUSEAU, Pink Panther II, 1964

Made in the USA
San Bernardino, CA
18 October 2015